lonely planet
food

AROUND THE WORLD
IN 80 FOOD TRUCKS

EASY & TASTY RECIPES FROM CHEFS ON THE ROAD

CONTENTS

🌱 *Vegetarian dishes*

INTRODUCTION

'Hey! What would you like today?'

Standing at the front of the line, you're ready to order. Your friends are behind you - one is holding a plate of Italian grilled octopus, the other a box of Thai chicken and rice. You opt for sizzling Korean soy noodles and veg. The owner promptly preps the dish - boiling, tossing, frying and drizzling right in front of you. The food goes from chopping board, to hot plate, to a steaming bowl of goodness in your hands in a matter of minutes. Your lunch is right here, and man it looks good.

In the past ten years, the culinary landscape of cities all over the world has been transformed by a new kind of street food purveyor: the gourmet food truck. Food trucks first rolled onto the scene in the US around the time of the last global financial crisis. (Many argue that the first of its form was renowned BBQ food truck Kogi (p140), based in Los Angeles.) It was an era when chefs were being laid off from traditional bricks-and-morter restaurants, and, with no job but a lot of talent and ambition, decided to take matters into their own hands. Combined with a growing number of festivals and a trend for pop-up attractions, the market was ripe for entrepreneurial cooks to make their mark in nomadic kitchens.

Today food trucks can be found on city streets from London to La Paz. With their gourmet plates served at street prices - and with no booking or dress code required - they cater to foodies who are more interested in taste than the formal trappings of restaurant life. Fun, local and affordable, they are also an easy way for urbanites to sample delicacies from the other side of the world and for visitors to get involved in a city's food scene.

For this book we've persuaded some of the world's most creative food truck chefs to share their recipes so that you can make them at home. From Indian-inspired paneer poutine to Lebanese spiced-chicken *msakhan*, the dishes feature everything from classics and family recipes to fusion concoctions inspired by travel experiences. Something they all have in common: they are very popular with a crowd.

Join us on a tour of the world's tastiest food truck dishes. Traverse each continent from west to east stopping off at 80 different trucks along the way, meet the chefs, and take a slice of their culinary creativity away with you.

So what are you waiting for? Go on, truck in!

Christina Webb

SPICY KILLARY LAMB SAMOSAS

with plum & apple chutney

MISUNDERSTOOD HERON, KILLARY, IRELAND

Run by husband-and-wife duo Kim and Reinaldo, Misunderstood Heron is located on the picturesque shores of Killary Fjord in Connemara, along Ireland's famous Wild Atlantic Way. Originally from Chile, Reinaldo travelled to Ireland to work as a kayak safety instructor, where he met Kim. The pair fell in love, and it wasn't long before they set off travelling together, exploring India on a motorcycle, as well as Nepal, Sri Lanka and Chile. Upon returning to Ireland, they sourced an affordable food truck that gave them the chance to create new dishes, as well as old family favourites from both Chile and Ireland. Using the finest local produce, their fare includes fresh mussels straight from the fjord; parsley and coriander falafel boxes; and stuffed empanadas. One of their most popular dishes, spicy lamb samosas, was inspired by their travels around India, and uses Killary lamb from a nearby farm.

Follow them on
Instagram: @misunderstood_heron
Facebook: www.facebook.com/MisunderstoodHeron

How to make it

MAKES 12 SNACK-SIZED SAMOSAS

Ingredients
½ tsp ground cumin
½ tsp coriander seeds
1 tsp turmeric powder
½ tsp cayenne pepper
1 tbs rapeseed oil
1 tsp mustard seeds
6 fresh curry leaves
1 large red onion, sliced
1½ garlic cloves, diced
1 *habañero* pepper, seeded &
    finely diced
250g (20oz) roasted lamb,
    chopped
125ml (4fl oz) boiling water
100g (3½oz) waxy potatoes,
    cooked al dente
4 filo pastry sheets
50g (1¾oz) butter, melted

For the chutney:
50ml (1¾fl oz) water
3 tbs soft brown sugar
¼ tsp ground cumin
1 plum, diced
1 medium red onion, cut into
    strips
1 medium cooking apple, diced
pinch of salt

Method
1. Place a large pan on a medium heat and dry-fry the cumin, coriander seeds, turmeric and cayenne for 2–3 minutes, until they release their aroma. Transfer to a plate.

2. Heat the oil over medium heat in the same pan, then add the mustard seeds and curry leaves. When the seeds begin to pop, add the onion, garlic and chilli, then the dry-fried spices. Cook for 10–15 minutes, until the onions have softened.

3. Add the lamb and heat through, then stir in the water and potatoes and set aside to cool.

4. Meanwhile, make the chutney. Put the water, sugar and cumin in a pan and heat until the sugar has dissolved. Add the plum, onion, apple and salt, stir to combine, and cook over low heat for about 20 minutes, stirring often, until the fruit has broken down and the liquid is thick. Transfer to a serving dish to cool.

5. Preheat the oven to 180°C (350°F).

6. Take one sheet of pastry (cover the remainder with a damp cloth) and, with the long edge facing you, brush the sheet lightly with melted butter. Cut the sheet horizontally into three sections.

7. Place 2 tbs of the filling on the left-hand edge of one of the strips and fold the top corner down over it. Flip the bottom left corner over to create a triangle. Continue folding until the end of the sheet, then place on a parchment-lined oven tray.

8. Repeat with the rest of the filo and filling.

9. Bake for 12–14 minutes until the samosas begin to go golden. Serve with the chutney.

SAN FRANCISCO LANGOUSTINE ROLL

HERMES' JOURNEY, A CORUÑA, SPAIN

Hermes Castro is a professional chef who worked in some of Spain's best restaurants for 13 years, including Michelin-starred Arzak in San Sebastián, before deciding to start his own food truck. His orange truck can be found in the northwestern coastal city of A Coruña, and at festivals and events throughout the region of Galicia. It offers classic street food, like filled baguettes and burgers, but with a gourmet twist, featuring quality ingredients such as fresh seafood from the nearby Atlantic Ocean. In 2018, the truck was awarded the second prize for Spain's best food truck at the Campeonato de España de Food Truck event. Their offerings include bratwurst sausage in a sesame bun, topped with pear chutney and yoghurt sauce; and chicken and goat's cheese in dark German bread, smothered in a spicy Thai-style sauce. Their most popular item? The San Francisco langoustine roll.

Follow them on
Instagram: @hermesjourney1
Facebook: www.facebook.com/hermesjourney

How to make it

SERVES 4

Ingredients
4 langoustines
4 brioche buns
30g (1¼oz) feta cheese
handful of microleaves

For the sauce:
1 red pepper, seeded & finely chopped
4 garlic cloves, finely chopped
4 tbs olive oil
5 tbs ketchup
2 tbs fried tomatoes
½ tsp jalapeño Tabasco sauce
½ tsp smoked chipotle Tabasco sauce

Method
1. Preheat oven to 100°C (212°F).

2. For the sauce, combine the pepper, garlic and olive oil in a roasting tray and cook for 30 minutes.

3. Add the rest of the sauce ingredients, reduce the oven temperature to 65°C (150°F), then place the langoustines in the sauce and cook for 1 hour.

4. When the sauce and langoustines are cooked, split and toast the brioche buns and spread with some sauce.

5. Peel the langoustines and put one in each bun, top with some feta cubes and microleaves and close the lid of the bun, adding more sauce if you like.

'It's a professional kitchen – we make everything from hamburgers to crayfish, always using seasonal produce and locally sourced ingredients where we can.'
Cayetano Gómez, owner

SEA BASS CEVICHE

with oysters

LACAYEJERA, SEVILLE, SPAIN

Meet Lacayejera, the famed Seville food truck owned by hotelier Cayetano Gómez. Having always enjoyed sampling food truck menus while living in the USA, Cuba and Switzerland, Gómez found it strange that Seville - a city with such great weather for eating outside - had no food truck scene. So, soon after he moved to the city, it became his ambition to bring street food to the Andalucian capital. Lacayejera is a play on Cayetano's name and the word *callejera* (something that lives or stays on the street), and his truck is now well known throughout Spain, as he was a finalist on the TV show *Cocineros al Volante* (Chefs at the Wheel). The bright-blue truck, decorated with the names of the dishes they serve, roams Seville and can be found in one of 12 locations. Cayetano and his team focus on fusion food, mixing Spanish ingredients into South American and Asian dishes. Popular choices include Asian burritos, tempura, and sea bass ceviche.

Follow them on
Instagram: @lacayejera
Facebook: www.facebook.com/lacayejera

How to make it

SERVES 2

Ingredients
1 small yuca (cassava)
1 small batata (white
    sweet potato)
180g (6oz) sea bass
    fillet, boned
1 tbs chopped coriander leaves
dash of sriracha chilli sauce
juice of 2 limes
4 oysters
½ a shallot, finely chopped
½ a red onion, finely sliced
salt & ground black pepper, to
    season
2 lime wedges, to garnish

Method
1. Boil or bake the yuca and batata until soft. Leave to cool.

2. Cut the sea bass fillet into 2cm (¾in)-wide fingers and do the same with the cooked yuca and batata.

3. Add the coriander, sriracha and lime juice to the mixture, stir to combine, then leave to marinate for 1 minute.

4. Place the ceviche mixture on a plate and place the oysters either side. Sprinkle with the shallots and red onion, season to taste and garnish with lime wedges.

'We have taken our *molletes* out of the street and into the *mano* (hand) of our food truck — hence the name La Manoleta.'
Maria Fernandez del Viso, co-owner

MOLLETE OF ROASTED PORK

with aioli potatoes & creamy mushrooms

LA MANOLETA, GIJÓN, SPAIN

La Manoleta is the brainchild of Maria Fernandez del Viso and Juanjo Bueno Lorenzo. With 10 years of experience in the food industry, they run a restaurant in the coastal city of Gijón in Asturias. As well as managing their small restaurant, the two decided to create a food truck to fuel their love of travelling around Spain. They also wanted as many people as possible to try their *molletes*. A speciality of La Manoleta, these are freshly baked Andalucian bread rolls with a base of fresh tomato and filled with various ingredients. One of their most popular offerings is a *mollete* filled with roasted pork, aioli potatoes and creamy wild mushrooms. Although based in Gijón, the bright silver flash of the La Manoleta caravan can be found at events and festivals all over the country.

Follow them on
Instagram: @lamanoleta

How to make it

SERVES 4

Ingredients
500g (1¼lb) Iberian pork cheek
2 red onions, chopped
1 green pepper, seeded & chopped
200ml (7fl oz) red wine
200ml (7fl oz) beef stock
salt & ground black pepper, to taste
100g (3¾oz) potatoes, peeled & cubed
30g (1¼oz) butter
2 tbs aioli or garlic mayonnaise
1 tbs olive oil
200g (7oz) *setas* (Spanish wild mushrooms), wiped clean & cut into strips
1½ garlic cloves, crushed
50ml (2fl oz) single cream
splash of cognac
4 *molletes* (or soft rolls), to serve
2 fresh tomatoes, chopped to a pulp

Method
1. Preheat the oven to 120°C (250°F). Place the pork in a deep, flameproof dish with one of the red onions, the green pepper, red wine, beef stock and seasoning.

2. Bring to the boil on the hob, then transfer to the oven and slow-roast for 6 hours.

3. Remove from the oven and leave to rest for 30 minutes before pulling the meat into pieces.

4. Meanwhile, boil the potatoes in a pan of salted water, until soft. Drain well, then add the butter and mash together. Stir in the aioli or garlic mayonnaise.

5. Heat the oil in a frying pan, then add the mushrooms with the remaining chopped red onion and the garlic and fry gently, until soft.

6. Flambé the mixture with a splash of cognac, then add the cream and season to taste.

7. Split and toast the *molletes*, then spread half with some tomato pulp, followed by the potato puree, pork, mushrooms and the top of the *mollete*.

PEMBROKESHIRE CRAB SALAD

CAFÉ MÔR, FRESHWATER WEST, UK

This solar-powered seafood deli is found hiding in an old fishing-boat-on-wheels tucked behind the glistening shoreline of Freshwater West beach, one of Pembrokeshire's most spectacular stretches of coastline. Now the proud owner of numerous awards - including Best Street Food or Takeaway (2014) and 'Best of the Best' at the British Street Food Awards (2011) - Jonathan Williams quit his desk job in 2010 and started Café Môr with a vision to celebrate an often-overlooked traditional Welsh ingredient: seaweed. Daily specials might include seaweed spaghetti with a laver bread pesto or a fresh Pembrokeshire crab and sea noodle salad, while menu classics like the bacon and laver bread butty or the lobster and laver bread roll keep the punters happy. The seaweed extravaganza doesn't stop there: rolls and burgers are topped with 'kelpchup', and each dish is seasoned with 'mermaid confetti' - sea salt crushed with dulse and wild coastal herbs.

Follow them on
Instagram: @beach_food
Facebook: www.facebook.com/PemBeachFood

How to make it

SERVES 2

Ingredients
1 carrot, grated
½ lime
1 tsp ginger puree
½ red chilli, finely chopped
dash of fish sauce
2 spring onions, chopped
handful of mixed salad leaves
1 large sprig of mint, leaves finely chopped
100g (3¾oz) freshly boiled crab meat, half brown, half white meat
handful of sea noodles or beanshoots
2 tbs seaweed chilli sauce or sweet chilli sauce
pinch of 'mermaid confetti' (or sea salt crushed with nori)
handful of pan-roasted peanuts

Method
1. In a large metallic bowl mix the grated carrot with the lime, ginger and chilli.

2. Add a dash of fish sauce, then add the spring onions, salad leaves and mint and toss to combine the ingredients.

3. Place the crab meat on top of the salad mix.

4. In a separate bowl, mix the sea noodles or beanshoots with the chilli sauce, then sprinkle over the crab meat and salad. Season with 'mermaid confetti' to taste and top with peanuts.

15

PIECE & CRAB

SHRIMPWRECK, GLASGOW, UK

ShrimpWreck is all about super fresh Scottish seafood - among the best in the world - served simply, quickly and cleverly. Started up by Ewen Hutchison in 2016, and usually based between Glasgow and Edinburgh at various markets and events, it has already won a word-of-mouth reputation for Scotland's best fish finger sandwich, and picked up the People's Choice accolade at the Scottish Street Food Awards in 2017. Signature dishes include shrimp buns loaded with battered king prawns and homemade Marie Rose sauce, fish tacos and chowders. Think seafood in a burger with all the trimmings.

Follow them on
Twitter: @ShrimpWreck
Facebook: www.facebook.com/shrimpwreck

How to make it

SERVES 2

Ingredients
vegetable oil, for deep frying
1 soft shell crab (Hotel size)
3–4 tbs plain flour, for dredging
2 brioche buns
coriander leaves

For the salsa:
2 tomatoes, cored & diced
1cm (½in) piece of cucumber,
    peeled and diced
½ mango, peeled and diced
½ red onion, finely diced
pinch of dried chilli
½ lime
small bunch of fresh coriander
pinch of salt

For the *togarashi* mayo:
4 tbs mayonnaise
togarashi seasoning, to taste
1 tsp mirin
1 tsp soy sauce
drop of sriracha chilli sauce

For the batter:
50g (2oz) plain flour
50g (2oz) cornflour
1 tsp baking powder
pinch of salt
150ml (¼ pint) ice-cold water

Method
1. Mix together all the salsa ingredients in a bowl. Set aside.

2. Combine all the mayo ingredients in a separate bowl. Set aside.

3. Combine all the dry batter ingredients in a large bowl, then gradually whisk in the water until the mixture has the consistency of double cream.

4. Heat the oil in a deep, heavy pan until it is hot enough that a cube of bread browns in about 45 seconds.

5. Carefully pick up the crab by the body, dip into flour, shake off the excess, then dip into the batter. Lift the crab out and shake off any excess batter.

6. Slowly lower the crab into the oil and fry for around 2 minutes on each side, until golden and crispy.

7. Remove with a slotted spoon or tongs and blot on kitchen paper, then cut in half.

8. Toast the brioche buns and assemble the crab piece as follows: brioche bottom, crab, spoonful of salsa, mayo and a few coriander leaves, brioche top. Repeat. Eat.

© RYAN MCGOVERNE

'Starting a food van was intended to be a stepping stone to the "real dream" of opening a cafe or restaurant... Now I can't see myself ever having a fixed location!'
Louise Abel, owner

WWW.THESPOTLESSLEOPARD.CO.UK

the spotless leopard it's our 6th birthday!

WWW.THESPOTLESSLEOPARD

VEG-AN FOOD

SUNDAY MARKET

VEGETABLE & CHICKPEA SHEPHERD'S PIE

THE SPOTLESS LEOPARD, BRISTOL, UK

The Spotless Leopard is run by founder Louise Abel in a converted Renault Master van. Her mission? To make beautiful, delicious, healthy, ethical food - and it's all vegan to boot. Louise started the business in 2012 after finishing a degree in fashion design; she's self-taught, and has mostly just learned on the job. And the experimenting continues to this day: from her regular pitch in Bristol, she dishes up an ever-changing menu that includes everything from protein-packed seitan steak sandwiches to hearty 'chilli non carne' - and some seriously decadent cakes. It's not just running a business and catering for crowds that have been an experience, though, it's also the array of events: the van has taken her to a medieval wedding where the bride was kidnapped during a Saxon invasion, a Gothic wedding atop a mountain in Wales, inside the ruins of a bombed cathedral, and many other wacky venues besides.

Follow them on
Instagram: @thespotlessleopard
Facebook: www.facebook.com/TheSpotlessLeopardUK

How to make it

🌿 SERVES 5–6

Ingredients
For the filling:
1 tbs rapeseed oil
1 large onion, diced
2 garlic cloves, minced
2 carrots, diced
1 celery stick, diced
leaves from 1 sprig of thyme
handful of green beans, chopped
few handfuls of frozen peas
small jar of sun-dried tomatoes, drained & finely chopped
1 tbs vegetable stock powder
400g (14oz) canned chopped tomatoes
100g (3¾oz) dried brown lentils
1 tbs yeast extract
400g (14oz) canned chickpeas
salt & ground black pepper, to taste

For the mash:
5 potatoes (mix of sweet & white), chopped
3 tbs vegan butter
salt, to taste

Method
1. Heat the oil a large pan, add the onion, garlic, carrots, celery and thyme and sauté for 10 minutes.

2. Add the green beans, peas, sun-dried tomatoes, stock powder, canned tomatoes, lentils, yeast extract and chickpeas, with the chickpea liquid and stir to combine.

3. Simmer for 30 minutes, until the lentils are soft, adding water if necessary. Season to taste.

4. Preheat the oven to 200°C (350°F).

5. For the mash, boil the potatoes in a pan. Once soft, mash with the butter and add salt to taste.

6. Fill two-thirds of a casserole with the filling, top with the mash and use a fork to mark stripes.

7. Bake for 30 minutes, until golden.

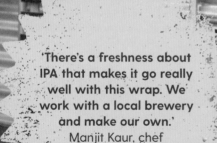

'There's a freshness about IPA that makes it go really well with this wrap. We work with a local brewery and make our own.'
Manjit Kaur, chef

PAKORA WRAP

with green chutney & carrot & coriander salad

MANJIT'S KITCHEN, LEEDS, UK

Food has always loomed large in Manjit Kaur's life. Growing up in Leeds, she recalls the Punjabi curries bubbling in vats in her Dad's garage during family gatherings. And when she started doing home deliveries from a secret kitchen at the end of 2010, it was a passion for food and these childhood memories, rather than any formal training in cookery, that inspired her to start a business feeding others. In the beginning, the entire business was driven by Twitter, with no physical base at all, but soon she graduated to a truck - the natural habitat for her grab-and-go take on authentic Punjabi cuisine - and helped launch what she calls 'the street food generation' in Leeds, amassing numerous accolades. Now with a permanent base in Kirkgate Market, Manjit offers a short menu of traditional *thalis*, baby-fist-sized onion bhajis and wraps, including a chilli paneer and this pakora version.

Follow them on
Instagram: @manjtskitchenuk
Twitter: @manjitskitchen

How to make it

🌿 SERVES 4

Ingredients
For the green chutney:
bunch of coriander
handful of mint
¼ white onion, finely chopped
juice of 1 lemon
1 tsp sugar
salt, to taste

For the carrot & coriander salad:
1 carrot, coarsely grated
1 small red onion, finely chopped
1 small bunch of coriander, chopped
squeeze of lime juice

For the pakoras:
4 onions, sliced
handful of spinach
1 medium potato, finely sliced
115g (4oz) gram/chick pea flour
25g (1oz) rice flour
1 tsp salt
1 tsp ground turmeric
1 tbs garam masala
1 tsp red chilli powder
150ml (5fl oz) oil, for frying

To serve:
4 large rotis, thin naan or tortillas
natural yoghurt
tamarind chutney or pickled red onion (optional)

Method
1. To make the green chutney, blend the ingredients in a blender with a little water until you reach a pesto-like consistency.

2. For the salad, mix everything together and set aside.

3. To make the pakoras, put the onions, spinach and potato in a bowl and mix by hand. Add the flour, and the dry spices and a little water and mix by hand until the vegetables are bound together in a thick batter.

4. Heat the oil in a deep pan until the surface shimmers. Working in batches, drop small clumps of the mixture into the oil and fry until golden. Remove with a slotted spoon and drain on kitchen paper.

5. Warm the rotis, naan or tortillas. Lay a line of the salad in the middle and top with 2–3 pakoras. Dress with green chutney, yoghurt, and tamarind chutney or pickled red onion, if using. Roll up and serve.

'Thailand – and its food – has played an enormous role in my life. I feel very lucky to make a living for myself and my family doing what I love. Plus I get to eat all the leftovers...'
Nic, Eadie, owner

PAD THAI NOODLES

with king prawns

THAIANGLE, BRIGHTON, UK

Nic Eadie pinpoints the moment he fell in love with Thai food as 8:30am on 11 December 1997 on the Khao San Road in Bangkok, where he enjoyed a green curry and a pad thai. Some 20 years later, these are now the most popular dishes at his vintage 1957 split-screen Citroën H food truck. When he returned from Thailand in 2004, he set out to learn to cook Thai food himself. A decade later, ThaiAngle was born, and a new chapter in Nic's life began. His food is all created from scratch, and includes everything from rich massaman curries to zesty Thai salads. Based near Brighton in Saltdean, it travels the South East and beyond for all manner of events. Outside of the summer months, they also run a pop-up takeaway from ThaiAngle HQ - as well as fitting in the occasional Thai cookery class.

Follow them on
Instagram: @thaiangle
Facebook: www.facebook.com/ThaiAngle

How to make it

SERVES 2

Ingredients
1 tbs vegetable oil
50g (2oz) extra-firm tofu, cut into
   small, rectangular pieces
1 carrot, sliced
1 small red onion, sliced
dried shrimp (optional)
1 egg
6 raw king prawns, unshelled
   and deveined
150g (5oz) rice noodles, soaked
   in cold water for at least 1 hour
2 lime wedges, to serve

For the pad thai sauce:
50g (2oz) palm sugar
25g (1oz) white sugar
3 tbs soy sauce
2 tbs tamarind concentrate

For the topping:
handful of crushed peanuts
2 spring onions (scallions), sliced
   thinly
chilli flakes
150g (5oz) beansprouts
handful of coriander leaves

Method
1. Make the sauce by melting together the sugars, soy sauce and tamarind in a pan.

2. Heat the oil in a wok, add the tofu and stir-fry for 1 minute. Add the carrot, onion and dried shrimp. Stir-fry for 30 seconds, then add the egg and scramble.

3. Add the prawns and stir-fry until starting to colour on both sides.

4. Push everything to one side. Add the noodles, spreading them out, then push the stir-fry on top.

5. Cook for about 30 seconds, moving the noodles so they don't stick. Once translucent, turn over and cook for 30 seconds more.

6. Stir in the sauce, then cook, stirring gently, until most of the sauce has been soaked up.

7. Add most of the peanuts, spring onion, chilli flakes and beansprouts. Mix a little, then turn off the heat.

8. Divide between two plates, and top with the remainder of the peanuts, spring onion and coriander, and the lime wedges.

BOB's *Lobster*

'I want to give a fun, fine-dining experience without any of the stuffiness. We're the only food truck that has sommeliers and a Front of House.'

Rob Dann, managing director

LOBSTER MAC 'N' CHEESE

BOB'S LOBSTER, LONDON, UK

'Seafood extravagance on a paper plate' is the BOB's Lobster tagline. Throw in some matched wines and the menu is a dream listing, including Ahi Tuna Tacos (sashimi tuna, wasabi guacamole, chipotle crema, sesame and wonton shell) and Lobster Rolls (steamed lobsters, herb mayonnaise, soft bun). MD Rob Dann imported the original lobster-red 1957 VW Camper van from Indiana, the logic being that it would have less rust, being from a landlocked state. Nine months of rebuilding later and Rob was discovering he had a lot to learn about food trucks... Prior to this, Rob had set up Bedales Wines in Borough Market in 2012, which he still oversees. BOB's ('Bedales of Borough') Lobster was initially an offshoot to get around the lack of kitchen at Bedales, but there are now two trucks and a permanent site (with the original truck inside) near London Bridge station.

Follow them on
Instagram: @bobs_lobster
Twitter: @BOBs_Lobster

How to make it

SERVES 4

Ingredients
2 x 450g (1lb) lobsters
5 large ripe tomatoes, chopped
1 white onion, chopped
2 carrots, chopped
½ bulb of garlic
4 tbs rapeseed oil
500ml (17fl oz) double cream
½ head of celery, chopped
½ tsp celery salt
½ tsp sweet paprika
3 sprigs of thyme
4 tbs lemon juice
300g (10½oz) dried macaroni pasta
100g (3½oz) grated cheddar cheese
50g (1¾oz) grated Parmesan
crispy fried shallots, to garnish
sweet herbs (chives, tarragon and marjoram), finely diced, to garnish

Method
1. Put 5cm (2in) water in a large pan and bring to the boil. Position a steamer insert above the water.

2. Kill the lobsters just prior to cooking (the best way is to stab the head). Place the tails inside the steamer. Cover and steam for 4–5 minutes, then remove to a bowl of iced water.

3. Once cold, crack the lobster and remove all the meat. Cut into large chunks and set aside.

4. Preheat the oven to 180°C (350°F). Mix half the lobster shells with the tomatoes, onion, carrots, garlic and oil. Roast for 45 minutes.

5. Transfer to a large pan on the lowest heat setting and add the cream, celery salt, paprika and thyme. Use a spoon or stick blender to break down the shells.

6. Simmer for 45 minutes, then pass through a fine sieve. Stir in the lemon juice.

7. Meanwhile, cook the pasta until al dente.

8. In an oven dish, combine the pasta, lobster, cheeses and sauce. Preheat a grill to high.

9. Grill for 5–10 minutes, until golden, then garnish with shallots and herbs.

GREAT BALLS OF FIRE PORK & BEEF MEATBALLS

THE BOWLER, LONDON, UK

 Jez Felwick gets a lot of chat in his meatball food truck. 'Literally every single day I get some banter about my balls.' Jez's background in television and branding, and his clever marketing - the truck is called The Bowler 'because it delivers a good ball' - means he's only got himself to blame. His AstroTurf-covered truck is also quite the sight. But Jez's road to meatball fame was gradual. He did a course at the Ballymaloe Cookery School in Ireland but it was a visit to LA in 2009 that introduced him to the gourmet food truck scene and planted a germ of an idea, hastened into action by a newsletter from Ballymaloe announcing a course on food trucks. He saw the 'premiumisation' of food like burgers and wanted to be the first to do meatballs. Given he's now got a published cookbook and Robert Downey Jr among his clientele, his ballsy decision seems to have paid off.

Follow them on
Twitter: @TheBowlerUK
Instagram: @thebowleruk

28

"When I saw the grass truck for sale, I rocked up to them and said "Oh man, this is a perfect, proper, showstopping, ridiculous beast of a kit. What's the story?""
Jez Felwick, founder

How to make it

SERVES 4–6

Ingredients
100g (3½oz) ricotta cheese
2 free-range eggs
400g (14oz) pork shoulder, finely minced
200g (7oz) beef chuck steak, finely minced
100g (3½oz) Japanese panko breadcrumbs (or fresh breadcrumbs)
2 garlic cloves, crushed
3 tbs coriander stems, finely chopped, leaves reserved
2 tsp sea salt
½ tsp dried chilli flakes
800ml (1.4 pints) spiced red onion & tomato sauce (or any tomato sauce)
sour cream, to serve
baby spinach, sliced pickled gherkin & rocket salad, to serve
brioche or burger buns, to serve

Method
1. Preheat oven to 220°C (425°F) and line a large baking tray with non-stick baking parchment.

2. Put the ricotta in a bowl and break up with a fork. Add the eggs and whisk together. Add the pork and beef, breadcrumbs, garlic, coriander stems, salt and chilli flakes. Mix with your hands until well combined.

3. Form about 18 balls, each 4–5cm (1½–2in) in diameter, packing each one firmly. Place on the baking tray.

4. Bake the meatballs for 15–18 minutes, turning the tray halfway through.

5. Meanwhile, heat the sauce in a large pan over medium heat.

6. When the balls are browned on top, add them to the sauce and simmer for 15 minutes.

7. Serve in toasted brioche or burger buns with sour cream and the salad, and sprinkle the coriander leaves and a few slices of pickled gherkin on top.

THE CHEESE TRUCK

GRILLED CHEESE:

✳ KEENS CHEDDAR, OGLESHIELD & ONION MIX

✳ ROSARY GOATS CHEESE, HONEY, WALNUT & ROSEMARY BUTTER

QUESO CHIHUAHUA CHEESE, RIZO & ROCKET

MELTING BRITISH | CHEESE | SINCE 2013

GRILLED CHEESE
CHEDDAR + O...
GOATS CHEESE, HONEY + WALNUTS
QUESO CHIHUAHUA ROCKET + CHORIZO

GOAT'S CHEESE, HONEY & WALNUT TOASTED SANDWICH

THE CHEESE TRUCK, LONDON, UK

Mastering the oozy art of melted sandwich fillings, The Cheese Truck's golden 1970s Bedford CF van is a welcome beacon for hungover eyes. Founder Mathew Carver had quit university to do a bit of music festival catering, but it wasn't until a 2013 trip to the USA, where he fell for the food truck scene, that an idea took hold. He realised the queues at grilled cheese trucks in particular were massive, and no one was doing anything like it in the UK. Starting with a stall at London's Maltby St Market in January 2014, a truck soon followed (Alfie), then another (Audrey). Fast-forward a few years and The Cheese Truck is catering for the likes of Tom Cruise's *Mission Impossible* wrap party, and Mathew has become a cheese expert, judging for numerous awards. His dedication to sourcing quality British cheeses sets the toasted sandwich bar high.

Follow them on
Twitter: @CheeseTruckLDN
Instagram: @thecheesetruck

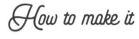

How to make it

🌿 SERVES 2

Ingredients
50g (1¾oz) good-quality salted butter
2 sprigs of fresh rosemary, leaves finely chopped
4 slices of sourdough bread
180g (6¼oz) soft fresh goat's cheese (The Cheese Truck uses Rosary goat's cheese from Salisbury, UK)
40g (1½oz) walnut pieces
50g (1¾oz) wild honey

Method
1. Melt the butter in a small pan, add the rosemary and leave to simmer on a low heat for 5 minutes. The butter should turn slightly green.

2. Lay out the bread and brush the butter on the outside of each slice.

3. Flip the bread over and spread the goat's cheese in a nice thick layer before adding the walnuts and honey. Add another slice of bread on top.

4. Heat a cast-iron skillet or a heavy frying pan on a low–medium heat.

5. Place the sandwich buttered side down in the skillet/pan and keep applying pressure or weight to the top while it's cooking. After about 4 minutes, flip the sandwich and cook on the other side.

6. When both sides are golden brown and the cheese is oozing out, you're done!

'We're inspired by trips we've made to the Middle East – we love discovering new flavours, bringing them back to London and putting our own twist on them.'
Gabriel Langford, co-owner

JERUSALEM SPICED CHICKEN

with onions in pomegranate molasses

LAFFA, LONDON, UK

Laffa started out life in 2015 when friends Gabriel and Ben quit their jobs and began food trucking in an old converted horsebox. Laffa's zingy wraps are a hit in London, where their two bright-blue vans roam between Flat Iron Square, the Street Feast night markets and summer festivals. Food is inspired by travels in Israel and Palestine and the smoky charcoal grills, spices and fresh-and-herby produce found on the streets of Tel Aviv and Jerusalem. Dishes feature a combo of grilled marinated meats, salads, slaw, sweet potato, aubergine and halloumi, all bundled up in a hot *laffa*, or flatbread, and drizzled with piquant sauces. Their most popular dish, Jerusalem Spiced Chicken, is a take on the mixed grills of Israel, and consists of chicken thighs cooked over coals and seasoned with onion and citrusy spices. It works brilliantly at a barbecue with salads, hummus and flatbread.

Follow them on
Instagram: @laffastreetfood
Facebook: www.facebook.com/laffastreetfood

How to make it

SERVES 4

Ingredients
8 boneless, skinless chicken
  thighs
pinch of sea salt
flatbread wraps, to serve
hummus, to serve
fresh lettuce, to serve

For the marinade:
2 tsp ground turmeric
1 tsp ground cumin
1 tsp ground coriander
1 tsp cracked black pepper
1 tsp sumac
4 garlic cloves, crushed
2 tbs natural yoghurt
1 tbs olive oil

For the onions:
3 red onions
3 tbs pomegranate molasses

Method
1. Combine all the marinade ingredients in a large bowl, add the chicken thighs and turn to coat. Cover and leave to marinate for at least 2 hours, but ideally overnight.

2. Cut the onions into wedges.

Fry on a medium-high heat in a heavy pan for 10 minutes or until golden brown, then add the pomegranate molasses, cover and turn the heat down low. Cook for a further 15 minutes until soft, sticky and sweet.

3. Meanwhile, set your grill to its highest setting (or even better, light the barbecue!). Season the chicken with salt and grill for 12–15 minutes, until golden and cooked through.

4. Let the chicken rest for 5 minutes, then carve into bite-sized pieces and mix with the onions and the resting juices.

5. Serve with flatbread wraps, hummus and fresh lettuce and let guests compile their own wraps.

FRIED CHICKEN

MOTHER CLUCKER, LONDON, UK

Reluctant heroes of London's early food truck scene, Ross Curnow and Brittney Bean met at a gig, circa 2008. What began as a search for a hangover cure (Brittney is from New Orleans and London's chicken offerings were not cutting it), grew legs when a designer mate created a 'Mother Clucker' poster and friends who tried the chicken starting asking them when they were 'opening'. A trip to Yorkshire saw them pick up an ex-US military ambulance (a 1996 Chevrolet Blazer), despite being terrified on the test drive. While it was being converted, they did a few pop-ups around London and catered for private parties. The punters clearly fell hard for Brittney's halal, NOLA-inspired recipe: the 'Cluck Truck' is now a permanent fixture at Old Truman Brewery, there are four Mother Clucker stalls around London, they make regular appearances at Field Day festival, and their first restaurant opened in Exmouth Market in 2018.

Follow them on
Instagram: @motherclucker
Twitter: @motherclucker

How to make it

SERVES 2

Ingredients
1 garlic bulb, minced
zest & juice of 2 lemons
2 chillies, finely chopped
handful of rosemary sprigs,
    finely chopped
2 chicken breasts, sliced into
    around 5 strips per breast
rapeseed oil for shallow-frying
    (or fill your deep-fryer)
100g (3½oz) plain flour
1 tbs paprika
½ tbs salt
½ tbs chilli/cayenne powder
50ml (1⅓fl oz) buttermilk
handful of flat leaf parsley,
    finely chopped, to serve

Method
1. Blend the garlic, lemon zest and juice, chillies and rosemary in a bowl. Mix in the chicken and marinate in the fridge for 1 hour.

2. Heat the oil in a frying pan or deep-fryer to 175°C (345°F).

3. Mix the flour, paprika, salt and chilli/cayenne powder in a large bowl.

4. Pour the buttermilk into a separate bowl.

5. Grab a handful of the chicken strips, dredge them in the flour mix to cover, then shake to remove any excess.

6. Drop the chicken into the buttermilk, then drop it back into the flour mixture and cover again.

7. Slowly place each strip of chicken in the oil. Cook for 3½ minutes, turning with tongs or shaking the deep-fryer basket every now and again.

8. Drain on kitchen paper and sprinkle with fresh parsley to serve.

'I try not to eat the chicken too often. I like to pretend I need to check it.'
Ross Curnow, co-founder

'When I emailed Rainbo about their advert looking for a new owner, I said "P.S. I'm the guy from Wilderness Festival". They immediately knew. I ate 60 of their gyozas that weekend.'
James Palmer, owner

CHICKEN, CHILLI & MISO GYOZA

with pickled mooli & dipping sauce

RAINBO, LONDON, UK

When food truck founders Ben Sheinwald and Xochi Balfour were serving financial adviser James Palmer his first homemade Rainbo gyoza at UK's Wilderness Festival in 2013, little did they know he would one day take over the business. James had been a fan of dumplings since childhood, when he loved eating grilled dumplings at a Chinese restaurant on family birthdays. From there his obsession progressed to gyoza and in 2016 he spotted Rainbo's ad for new owners and had a lightbulb moment. After spending six months learning the ropes, and a few freezing nights awaiting AA roadside service to fix the 1948 Ford pick-up (salvaged from a US scrap heap), James could not be happier. He gets to serve gyozas at London's food markets and UK festivals, as well as the Japanese street food that gave the truck its name. There's also a permanent site near London's Liverpool St station.

Follow them on
Instagram: @rainbofood
Twitter: @rainbofood

How to make it

MAKES 20

Ingredients
For the pickle:
350ml (12fl oz) water
350ml (12fl oz) rice vinegar
45ml (1½fl oz) mirin
75g (2½oz) sugar
2 tbs salt
½ tbs chilli flakes
20g (¾oz) fresh root ginger, grated
1 garlic clove, grated
20g (¾oz) mooli (daikon radish), thinly sliced
20g (¾oz) red cabbage, thinly sliced

For the gyozas:
100g (3½oz) chicken thigh mince
100g (3½oz) cabbage, finely chopped into 5mm (¼in) pieces
dash of chilli miso paste
pinch of salt
generous pinch of roasted sesame seeds
gyoza skins (shop bought)
vegetable oil, for frying

For the dipping sauce:
2 parts light soy sauce
2 parts mirin
1 part cooking sake

Method
1. For the pickle, put the water, vinegar, mirin, sugar, salt and chilli in a large pan on a high heat. Add the garlic and ginger and bring to the boil. Lower the heat and simmer for 20 minutes.

2. Allow to cool, then add the mooli and red cabbage and pickle for at least 24 hours.

3. Combine all the dipping sauce ingredients and set aside.

4. Combine the chicken, cabbage, miso, salt and sesame seeds.

5. Fill each gyoza skin with 1–2 tsp of this mixture. Gently fold over, pinch one corner together and fold the skin on to itself until the filling is fully encased.

6. Heat some oil in a frying pan. Place each gyoza in the pan flat side down, add a sprinkle of water and cover with a lid.

7. Check every few minutes, adding a little water when necessary. Cook for 4–6 minutes, until crispy on the bottom and the skin is translucent on the top, then serve with the pickle and sauce.

ASPARAGUS, EWE'S CHEESE, MOZZARELLA & HAZELNUT PIZZA

WELL KNEADED, LONDON, UK

Established in 2011, this food truck hopes to simultaneously bring communities together through wood-fired pizza and help change them. Founders Bridget Goodwin and Laurence Callaghan met while doing youth work in Romania and have partnered with a youth charity in southwest London called E:merge. And if you seek out their vintage red Citroën van, you'll find crispy pizza with (mostly) organic, British seasonal toppings made by an intern trained in all aspects of the business. The sourdough is made with bee pollen in the starter, which gives it a healthy sweetness. There is usually a vegan option, along with seasonal spins, such as the Christmas special involving Brussels sprouts, smoked pork jowl and a béchamel and chestnut roux base. The van parks regularly around London and at festivals.

Follow them on
Twitter: @wellkneadedfood
Instagram: @wellkneadedfood

How to make it

🌿 MAKES 2 PIZZAS

Ingredients
For the naturally leavened dough:
200g (7½oz) type 00 flour
250g (8½oz) Canadian strong flour
150ml (5fl oz) water (use tepid in winter, cold in summer)
½ tbs sourdough starter (you need to make this well in advance)
½ tbs salt

For the topping:
splash of garlic oil
handful of chopped asparagus
60g (2oz) ewe's cheese (Well Kneaded use Wigmore)
70g (2½oz) fior di latte or mozzarella
sprinkle of chopped, roasted hazelnuts
handful of rocket

Method
1. Combine the flours, water and starter until you have a 'scrappy heap' of rough dough. Cover and leave to stand at room temperature for 45 minutes.

2. Add the salt and knead the dough for 3 minutes. Let it rest for 2 minutes then knead for another 3 minutes.

3. Leave to rest at an ambient temperature for about 30 minutes, then ferment it for a further 36–48 hours in the fridge. About halfway through, divide it into two 200g (7oz) dough balls.

4. When you're ready to cook, bring the dough to room temperature. Fire up your pizza oven (or preheat your normal oven to its highest temperature).

5. Flour a surface and roll out each dough ball into an oval shape.

6. Drizzle the garlic oil over each base, then add the toppings.

7. Cook for around 7 minutes, until the top starts to brown. Top with the rocket and serve.

'We only use the best part of the pork for our *botifarra*, without additives, and source our meat from farms where the ethical treatment of animals is rigorous.'
Pilar Carnicer, co-owner

CATALAN SAUSAGE

with white bean hummus

MR FRANK AND THE BUTIS, BARCELONA, SPAIN

Mr Frank and the Butis opened in 2011 and was the first food truck in Barcelona, as well as a pioneer of the street food movement in Spain. Owners Ignasi Bisbe, Mar Carnicer and Pilar Carnicer had been inspired by their travels to cities such as San Francisco, Paris and Berlin, where trucks had already made their mark, and wanted to establish Catalan street food. In 2013, they took things one step further and created Van Van, a gastronomic street food market with various trucks, which move around to city festivals and events. Their menu focuses on the traditional Catalan pork sausage, a *botifarra*, and pairs it with Mediterranean ingredients such as dried tomatoes, *sobrassada* (cured spiced sausage paste from the Balearic Islands), honey and Brie. The truck's most popular offering is the Butimon, their take on the traditional Catalan dish - *botifarra amb seques*, a grilled pork sausage served with braised white beans.

Follow them on
Instagram: @mrfrankandthebutis
Facebook: @mrfrankandthebutis

How to make it

SERVES 4

Ingredients
4 *botifarra* sausages, 150g (5oz) each (or use chunky pork sausages)
4 pieces of rustic white baguette or Mediterranean-style bread
lamb's lettuce leaves

For the white bean hummus:
500g (1¼lb) white beans, such as cannellini or haricot
½ garlic clove
½ tsp tahini
glug of olive oil
pinch of salt
pinch of paprika
squeeze of lemon
about 120ml (4fl oz) water

Method
1. Fry or grill the sausages until golden and cooked through.

2. Meanwhile, put all the hummus ingredients apart from the water in a blender. Whizz them all up together, adding the water slowly as you go, until it becomes a smooth and creamy paste.

3. Split open the bread and place the sausage inside with some leaves of lamb's lettuce.

4. Spoon the white bean hummus on top of the *botifarra* and serve.

41

RESTOMOBIL &
Produits bio, loc

MOZZARELLA & TARTUFATA FRENCH TOAST

EL CAMION, BRUSSELS, BELGIUM

On a boozy Brussels' night in 2008, three friends agreed they wanted to eat a different kind of street food, so they found an old dentist wagon from 1973 and El Camion was born. Among the first food trucks in Belgium, the mobile joint is now run by Joël Geismar, one of the three founding friends and chef at the much-acclaimed restaurant Garage-à-Manger. El Camion serves Italian and Belgian recipes street-food style. Those fond of American fast cuisine can come on board the truck and ask for an asparagus-mushroom-mayo hot dog, while diners in the mood for Belgian classics can try the *mitraillette* with confit of duck (*mitraillette* is a sandwich jam-packed with meat and fries, one of Belgium's culinary oddities). With almost 10 years under the wheels, Joël uses organic, local and seasonal produce to make top-notch dishes. The truck might be old scrap, but it's a Brussels' food truck Rolls-Royce.

Follow them on
Facebook: www.facebook.com/elcamionfoodtruck

How to make it

🌿 SERVES 4

Ingredients
oil, for deep-frying
1 egg
130ml (4½fl oz) milk
70g (2½oz) fresh breadcrumbs
4 large slices of white bread
3 tbs *tartufata* (Italian sauce made from truffles, mushrooms and black olives)
170g (6oz) fior di latte or mozzarella
salt & ground black pepper
fleur de sel, to serve

Method

1. Put the oil in a deep-fryer or large, heavy pan and heat to 180°C (350°F).

2. Beat together the egg and milk in a shallow dish.

3. Put the breadcrumbs in a large, flat dish.

4. Spread each bread slice with *tartufata*.

5. Slice the fior di latte or mozzarella and lay on half of the bread slices.

6. Add salt and pepper to taste, then close the sandwiches with the remaining bread slices.

7. Cut the sandwiches diagonally into 4 triangles.

8. Dunk each triangle in the egg-milk mixture, soaking both sides.

9. Press each soaked triangle into the breadcrumbs, coating them well.

10. Fry the triangles for 3 minutes, until golden.

11. Drain on kitchen paper and sprinkle with some fleur de sel to serve.

WATERMELON-MINT ICE POPS

NANOUK, BRUSSELS, BELGIUM

From the cold world of bank marketing to the frozen emporium of ice pops, Christine's life seems to have dropped on the Celsius scale but her ice pops are the hottest in town. It was on a 2013 trip to Italy that she fell in love with the icy treats and decided to quit her desk job and turn her life around. An important motivation behind her new career choice: creating healthy nibbles for her kids by making ice pops with only natural ingredients and as little sugar as possible. Finding inspiration in cocktail lists and botanical books, her creativity has led her to concoct more than 100 recipes over the years. From pineapple-ginger to cardamom-chocolate all the way through beer, there's virtually nothing she can't turn into a delicious pop. Euphoric kids and adults alike, everybody is hooked. Even dogs...

**Follow them on
Facebook:** www.facebook.com/nanoukicepops

How to make it

🌿 **SERVES 8**

Ingredients
½ watermelon
250ml (8fl oz) water
125g (4¼oz) sugar
12 fresh mint sprigs, plus 20 leaves
1 mint herbal teabag
4g (⅛oz) agar-agar
1 tsp lemon juice

Method
1. Skin, seed and chop the watermelon, then blitz in a blender to obtain 1L (1¾ pints) of juice.

2. Put the water and sugar in a pan and heat gently until the sugar dissolves and a syrup forms. When the temperature reaches 102°C (215°F), remove from the heat and add the mint sprigs and teabag. Leave to infuse and cool for 1 hour.

3. Remove the mint and teabag and heat the syrup to 60°C (140°F).

4. Add the agar-agar, watermelon juice, mint leaves and lemon juice.

5. Cook for 3 minutes, then leave to cool.

6. Churn in an ice-cream maker.

7. Fill ice pop moulds with the mixture and leave to freeze overnight.

45

LEMON WAFFLES

with blueberries & mascarpone cream

WAFELTJES VAN ONS BOMMA, ANTWERP, BELGIUM

Before he started wielding his waffle machine under an umbrella 13 years ago, Wes used to work in advertising. Tired of the bling, he quit his job and decided to put his dexterous hands to good use: making waffles. He duly upgraded his shabby table stand into a white old Mercedes truck and started selling more than 30 types of seasonal waffles, from summery lemon to wintertime ginger. His following grew so exponentially that he soon acquired a second black truck and is about to get a third. Wafeltjes van ons Bomma means 'Little waffles from our granny' in Flemish, and it just so happens that Wes's grandma did play a pivotal role in the story: she used to live next door and would sell bread and pastries at the local market, and spent years teaching young Wes how to bake pancakes, cakes and ... waffles!

Follow them on
Instagram: @WafeltjesVanOnsBomma
Facebook: www.facebook.com/wafeltjesvanonsbomma

How to make it

🍃 SERVES 6

Ingredients
For the mascarpone cream:
250g (8oz) mascarpone
120ml (4fl oz) double cream
75g (3oz) icing sugar
½ tsp vanilla extract

For the waffles:
250g (9oz) self-raising flour
pinch of salt
35g (1¼oz) sugar
2 eggs, separated
cooking spray or vegetable oil,
    for greasing
250ml (8fl oz) milk
1 tsp vanilla extract
125g (4¼oz) melted butter
juice of ½ lemon
grated zest of 1 lemon

To serve:
lemon slices
icing sugar
250g (9oz) fresh blueberries

Method
1. To make the mascarpone cream, combine all the ingredients. Set aside in the fridge.

2. For the waffles, mix together the flour, salt and sugar in a large bowl. Grease and preheat a waffle iron.

3. In a separate bowl, beat the egg whites until fluffy.

4. Pour the milk, egg yolks, vanilla extract and melted butter into the flour mixture. Gently combine all ingredients until smooth. Whisk in the lemon juice and zest.

5. Gently fold in the stiff egg whites with a large spatula.

6. Ladle some batter into the waffle iron and cook until golden. Remove to a plate and repeat until all the batter is used up.

7. While the waffles are cooking, caramelise the lemon slices in a hot griddle pan for a few minutes.

8. Serve the waffles lukewarm, dusted with icing sugar, with a dollop of mascarpone cream, lots of blueberries and a slice of caramelised lemon.

47

BELL PEPPER & TUNA PANZEROTTI

BIO PAN 08, LUXEMBOURG CITY, LUXEMBOURG

Pietro and Analivia left Italy and moved to Luxembourg almost a decade ago in pursuit of a prosperous future in the banking sector. Disenchanted and unwilling to sacrifice their private life for dough, they opted for a radical career change. After a series of handy jobs, from electrical works to butcher's assistant, the 40-something couple finally decided to get their hands dirty and start their own business: a panzerotti food truck (panzerotti are small, fried half-moon-shaped calzone). Their nonna's pizza recipe is their most valued heirloom and so the pair dug out childhood memories of gargantuan family feasts in Southern Italy to create their organic panzerotti recipes. The peperonotto panzerotti is made with bell pepper, while their gorgonzottos are made with ... you guessed it, Gorgonzola! Sweet-toothed rascals can relish a limonotto (ricotta, lemon curd and pine nuts) and many more half-moon treats involving fruity jams and nutty spreads.

Follow them on
Facebook: www.facebook.com/biopan08

How to make it

SERVES 4

Ingredients
For the dough:
250ml (8fl oz) milk
12g (½oz) fresh yeast
250g (9oz) plain flour, plus extra for dusting
250g (9oz) semolina
3 tbs olive oil, plus extra for greasing
10g (¼oz) salt

For the filling:
2 tbs olive oil
2 red peppers, peeled, seeded & cut into thin strips
2 yellow peppers, peeled, seeded & cut into thin strips
1 onion, cut into thin strips
1 garlic clove, finely chopped
150g (5oz) canned tuna, drained
300g (11oz) grated mozzarella
pinch of dried oregano
100ml (3½fl oz) tomato puree
salt, to taste
oil, for deep-frying

Method
1. For the dough, heat the milk until blood temperature, add the yeast and stir to dissolve.

2. In a bowl, mix the flour, semolina, oil, salt and yeast mixture until a sticky ball forms.

3. Knead on a floured surface for 10 minutes, until smooth, adding a little flour as needed.

4. Transfer to an oil-coated bowl, cover and leave to rise for 4 hours in a warm place.

5. Heat the oil in a frying pan, add the peppers, onion and garlic and sauté for 10 minutes.

6. Add the tuna, mozzarella, oregano, tomato puree, salt to taste and leave to cool.

7. Put oil in a deep-fryer or deep pan and preheat to 190°C (375°F).

8. Knead the dough briefly, then stretch it on a floured surface until thin. Cut out eight 15cm (6in) circles.

9. Place a large tablespoon of filling in the centre of each, fold into a half-moon shape and press to seal the edges.

10. Deep-fry each for 3 minutes on each side until golden. Drain on kitchen paper and serve hot.

49

'Eating should be about sharing a moment.'
Pierre, owner and chef

www.HOPLA-FOOD.fr

LOCAL FOOD COMPANY

CARPACCIO FLAMMEKUECHE

HOPLA FOOD, STRASBOURG, FRANCE

In his early 30s, Pierre is a fervent Alsatian culinary ambassador and still cherishes childhood memories of his grandfather taking him and his siblings to the bakery down the street to get freshly baked pretzels. In 2013, Pierre realised there was not much on offer when it came to Alsatian street food, so he found a Renault Master and turned it into Hopla Food. 'Hopla geiss' is a traditional Alsatian expression, which means 'Come on, sheep!', but nowadays it is mostly used to say 'Come on!' or 'Let's go'. It fits this food truck concept like a glove, as Pierre is all about fast Alsatian classic recipes with a twist. He has now extended his fleet to two trucks and a vintage food bike, serving pretzel burgers, *grumbeerekiechle* (the regional take on potato rösti) and *flammekueches*, which translates as 'cakes on fire' - a pizza-meets-quiche concoction. Traditionally, the thin-crusted speciality is served with a generous layer of sour cream, sprinkled with onions and bacon.

Follow them on
Instagram: @hoplafood
Facebook: www.facebook.com/HoplaFood

How to make it

SERVES 4–6

Ingredients
For the dough:
225g (8oz) plain flour, plus extra for dusting
3 tbs olive oil, plus extra for greasing
1 tsp salt
150ml (¼ pint) tepid water

For the topping:
115g (4oz) sour cream
½ tsp salt
½ tsp nutmeg
juice of ½ lemon
200g (7oz) beef carpaccio
2 tbs olive oil
handful of rocket leaves
fleur de sel, to taste

Method
1. Preheat the oven to 200°C (400°F). Flour a baking sheet and put it in the oven.

2. For the dough, combine the flour, oil and salt in a large bowl. Slowly add 120ml (4fl oz) water and stir to combine. Add just enough of the remaining water to form a soft dough.

3. Knead on a lightly floured surface for about 10 minutes, until smooth. Place in an oiled bowl and cover with clear film. Leave to rest for 30 minutes.

4. For the topping, combine the sour cream, salt and nutmeg in a small bowl. Taste and adjust the seasoning as needed.

5. Divide the dough into 4–6 equal parts and roll each of them out on a floured surface into a very thin oval or rectangular shape.

6. Working in batches, spread some of the cream on the bases, sprinkle with lemon juice and transfer to the preheated baking sheet.

7. Bake for 3 minutes or until they start to scorch on the edges.

8. Top with carpaccio, olive oil, rocket leaves and some fleur de sel.

'Not only was there (at the time) not any good authentic Indian food around, no one was doing anything different either, and hence Chai Wallahs was born, specialising in Indian fusion food.'

Oliver Wakeham, owner

INDIAN-STYLE POUTINE

CHAI WALLAHS, BERLIN, GERMANY

Seeing a gap in the Berlin street food scene, Chai Wallahs' founder Oliver Wakeham decided to draw on his experiences travelling and learning from chefs in India to open a stall at the famous Markthalle Neun street food market in 2014. Oliver fused Indian flavours with Western concepts and the demand for the unique dishes exploded, so Chai Wallahs set out to customise an old East German caravan to take the food on the road. They quickly outgrew the small camping vehicle and started work on the iconic Chevrolet P20 step van that now has locals queuing around the clock for a taste of their exciting dishes. Chai Wallahs create their showstopping Indian-style poutine with homemade paneer cheese, hand-cut fries and the juices from their slow-roasted pork belly, but this recipe can easily be recreated with store-bought items and pantry staples.

Follow them on
Instagram: @Chaiwallahsberlin
Facebook: www.facebook.com/Chaiwallahsberlin

How to make it

SERVES 4

Ingredients
100ml (3½fl oz) rapeseed oil
3 garlic cloves
1 bird's-eye chilli
1cm (½in) piece of fresh root ginger
1 bunch of coriander
2 tbs garam masala
2 tbs Madras curry powder
1 tsp ground turmeric
1L (1¾ pints) pork stock
250ml (8fl oz) water
1 spring onion, sliced
1 lime
500g (1¼lb) paneer, cubed
salt & ground black pepper, to taste

For the fries:
2 large russet or Maris Piper potatoes
2L (3½ pints) vegetable oil
salt, to taste

Method
1. Heat the oil in a heavy pan over medium heat. Pound or blitz the garlic, chilli and ginger into a paste. Add to the oil and sauté until fragrant.

2. Reserving the leaves, finely chop the coriander stalks and add to the oil with the garam masala, Madras powder and turmeric. Cook for 5 minutes, stirring constantly.

3. Add the pork stock and water and scrape any sticky pieces from the bottom of the pan. Reduce the heat and simmer for 30 minutes, until thick. Season to taste.

4. For the fries, cut the potatoes into strips and soak in cold water for 30 minutes. Heat the oil in a deep, heavy pan to 140°C (275°F). Drain the potatoes and dry with kitchen paper, then fry in the oil for 5 minutes. Remove and drain on kitchen paper.

5. Bring the oil to 180°C (350°F). Fry the potatoes again for 5–6 minutes, until crispy and golden. Drain on kitchen paper and season.

6. To serve, pour the sauce over a portion of fries and add a handful of the paneer cubes. Top with roughly chopped coriander leaves, the sliced spring onions and a squeeze of lime.

KÄSSPÄTZLE

HEISSER HOBEL, BERLIN, GERMANY

Kässpätzle is a dish from the South German area of Swabia, and has spread across several regions, thanks to its simplicity. Often likened to mac 'n' cheese, it consists of fresh noodles tossed in cheese and served up with crispy fried onions. Although they only sell one dish, the folks behind Heisser Hobel have become locally renowned in Berlin because of their exclusive cheese blend, which was developed in a small dairy and uses local milk to create nine-month aged Allgäuer Bergkäse and four-month aged Emmental. Operators Florian, Myriam and Oliver are considered early pioneers of the German food truck movement, having converted a Soviet-era German camper (known as a 'Nagetusch') into a rolling kitchen in April 2013. Despite battling temperatures of 50°C (122°F) during the summertime, the chefs say they love the freedom that comes with a mobile kitchen and the sense of community in the food truck scene.

**Follow them on
Instagram: @heisserhobel**

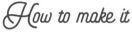

How to make it

🌿 SERVES 2

Ingredients
For the *spätzle* noodles:
350g (12oz) plain flour
2 eggs
625ml (22fl oz) water
2 tsp salt

For the onions:
1 small onion
1 tbs flour
pinch of paprika
45g (1½oz) butter

To serve:
100g (3½oz) grated Emmental
    cheese, or another cheese of
    your choice
handful of chives, snipped
freshly ground black pepper

Method

1. To make the noodles, combine the flour, eggs, water and salt in a bowl and stir until it forms a thick but slightly fluid dough.

2. Set aside while you bring a large pan of salted water to the boil over high heat.

3. Finely slice the onions into rings and dust with the flour and paprika.

4. Melt the butter in a frying pan over medium-high heat and add the onions, frying until golden. Drain on kitchen paper and leave to become crispy after they cool.

5. Divide the cheese between six serving bowls.

6. When the water is boiling, place a colander with large holes or a *spätzlehobel* over the top, then fill with your *spätzle* dough.

Use a rubber spatula or plastic scraper to help push your *spätzle* through the holes into the water.

7. Wait for the *spätzle* to float, then allow to cook for 1 minute more before removing from the water and placing directly into each bowl of cheese. Stir vigorously until the cheese is completely melted.

8. Serve topped with the fried onions, chives and pepper.

BUTTERMILK-FRIED-CHICKEN BISCUIT SANDWICHES

with honey butter

HUMBLE PIE, BERLIN, GERMANY

Humble Pie's Sarah Durante has been serving Southern comfort food to Berliners since 2015, bringing the flavours she learned from her family kitchen to the streets of Germany. With a menu featuring seasonal sweet pies, flaky buttermilk biscuits and crunchy Nashville-style chicken, hungry visitors from all walks of life can get a taste of the American south from this trailer, which can be found at various events across Berlin. Having always enjoyed preparing food, Durante started her business when she was inspired by Berlin's 'try-it-out' culture. Having partnered with local street food legends such as Fraulein Kimchi and local beer vendors Two Fellas for one-off events, Durante's attitude means local fans will always have the chance to try a new take on their favourite comfort food dishes.

Follow them on
Instagram: @humblepieberlin
Facebook: www.facebook.com/humblepieberlin

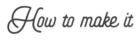

How to make it

SERVES 5

Ingredients

For the chicken:
250ml (8fl oz) buttermilk
1 tbs hot sauce
½ tsp salt
¼ tsp ground black pepper
¼ tsp cayenne pepper
5 boneless, skinless chicken thighs
175g (6oz) plain flour
40g (1½oz) cornflour
1 tbs garlic powder
1 tbs onion powder
1 tbs paprika
2 tsp cayenne pepper
½ tbs salt
peanut or vegetable oil, for frying (enough to fill your pan about two-thirds full)

For the biscuits:
275g (10oz) plain flour, plus extra for dusting
1 tbs baking powder
¾ tsp salt
½ tsp sugar
75g (3oz) butter, cubed & frozen for 10–15 minutes
250ml (8fl oz) buttermilk

For the honey butter:
50g (2oz) unsalted butter, room temperature
2 tbs honey
¼ tsp salt

Method

1. For the chicken, combine the buttermilk, hot sauce, salt, pepper and cayenne, add the chicken and mix well. Cover and marinate in the fridge overnight.

2. To prepare the honey butter, cream everything together. Chill until needed.

3. To prepare the biscuits, preheat the oven to 220°C (425°F).

4. Place the flour, baking powder, salt and sugar into a food processor with the butter and pulse until it has combined and is crumbly.

5. Remove the blade and add the buttermilk, stirring just enough to incorporate all the dry bits.

6. Turn out the dough on to a floured work surface and dust with a little extra flour. Roll the dough to 5mm (¼in), then fold it and roll it out again. Gently

repeat this process twice to ensure a flaky, buttery biscuit.

7. Using a floured 7.8cm (3½in) round cookie cutter, stamp out the biscuits and place close together on a baking tray lined with baking parchment.

8. Bake for 20–25 minutes, until golden and cooked.

9. Prepare the flour dredge for the chicken by combining the flour, cornflour, garlic and onion powder, paprika, cayenne pepper and salt in a bowl. Remove the chicken from the fridge.

10. Heat the oil to 180°C (350°F) over a medium heat in a deep, heavy pan.

11. Place each piece of chicken into the flour, dabbing it to ensure an even coating. Fry each piece for 5–8 minutes, taking care not to overcrowd the pan.

12. Set the cooked chicken on a wire rack to drain.

13. Split each biscuit and liberally spread some honey butter on each half. Add a piece of chicken to each. Try dousing the chicken in hot sauce for an extra kick!

SUPER CHEDDAR BURGER

with red onion jam

PANEER, BUDAPEST, HUNGARY

Hungarian food is heavy on the meat, but lacto-vegetarians can usually reach for the fried cheese. Those who want to try a modern take on this classic Hungarian dish should head over to the Paneer food truck at Karavan Street Food Court next to the famous ruin pub Szimpla Kert. Paneer - a play on the Hindi word for cheese and the Hungarian word *panírozott*, meaning 'breaded' - first opened its food truck here in 2014. Initially they sold breaded and fried pieces of local Trapista cheese, along with Cheddar, Camembert and Maci - a local cream cheese wedge - but when Paneer started taking food trucks to the festival scene a new snack was born: the Real Cheese Burger. This is essentially a burger that replaces a meat patty with fried cheese, and the the Super Cheddar Burger is especially delicious, combining a ciabatta bun, with fried onions and homemade steak sauce.

Follow them on
Facebook: www.facebook.com/pg/paneerbudapest

58

How to make it

SERVES 4

Ingredients
4 ciabatta rolls
4 x 100g (3½oz) thick slices of
    Cheddar cheese
about 6 tbs flour
2 eggs, beaten
75g (3oz) breadcrumbs
oil, for deep-frying
75g (3oz) rocket

For the steak sauce:
150g (5oz) ketchup
50g (2oz) mustard
400ml (14fl oz) stock
10 peppercorns
8 garlic cloves
100g (3½oz) honey
pinch of salt

For the fried onions:
250g (9oz) red onions
pinch of salt
3–4 tbs flour
500ml (17fl oz) oil, for shallow-frying

For the red onion jam:
100g (3½oz) granulated sugar
500g (1¼lb) red onions, sliced
2 tsp red wine vinegar
200ml (7fl oz) balsamic vinegar
salt, to taste

Method

1. Make the steak sauce. Put all the ingredients into a pan, bring to the boil and cook until it reduces to two-thirds of the volume. Strain and set aside.

2. To make the fried onions, slice the onions into fine rings, season with salt and coat with flour. Heat the oil in a frying pan over a medium-high heat, add the onions and fry until golden. Drain on kitchen paper and set aside.

3. To make the red onion jam, put the sugar in a pan over medium heat and fry to caramelise. Add the onions and vinegars, then sauté until the onion softens into a jam-like consistency. Add salt to taste.

4. Slice the ciabatta rolls and toast lightly.

5. Cover the cheese slices in flour, dip in the beaten egg and roll in breadcrumbs.

6. Heat the oil in a deep, heavy pan until it is hot enough that a cube of bread browns in 45 seconds. Lower in the cheese slices and fry until golden.

7. Spread some onion jam on the bottom half of each ciabatta roll, then add rocket, cheese and fried onion. Drizzle over steak sauce and close.

TURKEY BURGER

with sauteed fennel & crispy fried onions

STREET CHEFS, SOFIA, BULGARIA

The idea for starting Street Chefs was first born in 2014 when friends Petko and Dimitar decided to escape the real-estate business and follow their passion for food. The duo travelled to New Mexico to buy a classic Airstream caravan and bring it back to Sofia, and it then took them a year to transform it into a professional kitchen and to develop their recipes. On a lucky Friday 13th in 2015, Sofia's first food truck officially opened its doors at one of the city's iconic central corners. The concept is simple: genuine, affordable food made in front of customers' eyes. The menu features ten burgers - including the hit chef's option with beef and bacon; salmon with cream sauce and chives; and a veggie burger with cauliflower and chickpeas. Meat is cooked on a slow fire, sauces are homemade, and brioche buns are freshly baked across the street.

Follow them on
Instagram: @street.chefs
Facebook: www.facebook.com/street.chefs.bulgaria

How to make it

SERVES 4

Ingredients
100ml (3½fl oz) coconut milk
100g (3¾oz) ready-made Thai red curry paste
800g (1¾lb) skinless turkey breast fillets
250ml (8fl oz) vegetable oil
2 onions, very finely sliced
salt, to taste
½ fennel bulb, sliced
4 jalapeño peppers, finely chopped
250g (9oz) mayonnaise
juice of ½ a lemon
ground black pepper, to taste
4 brioche buns, split in half and toasted, to serve
4 iceberg lettuce leaves, to serve

Method
1. Mix the coconut milk and curry paste in a large bowl, add the turkey breast fillets and stir to coat. Leave to marinate for 30 minutes if possible.

2. Preheat the oven to 180°C (350°F). Put the turkey in a roasting tray and cover with foil, then roast for about 40 minutes, until cooked through.

3. Leave to rest for 10 minutes, then cut into thin slices.

4. Heat the oil in a wok or deep frying pan, add the onions and cook until golden brown and crispy. Add salt to taste and drain on a plate lined with kitchen paper.

5. Remove the turkey from the roasting tray, then add to the pan with the roasting tray juices, along with the fennel. Stir over a medium heat for 2–3 minutes to warm through.

6. Combine the jalapeño peppers with the mayonnaise and season with lemon juice, salt and pepper.

7. To serve, smear some of the mixture on the cut sides of the brioche buns. Add a leaf of iceberg lettuce, turkey slices and crispy fried onions to taste.

FOREST PANCAKE

BELKI&UGLEVODY, ST PETERSBURG, RUSSIA

 Belki&Uglevody started in 2015, but the idea was born a few years earlier, when the concept of food trucks was new to Russia. It was opened by a group of friends, led by Pavel, who is now head chef. Throughout his childhood, Pavel watched his relatives cooking and began to help them, realising this was what he wanted to do in life. Today, Belki&Uglevody is one of the most successful food trucks in St Petersburg, usually found at summer food and music festivals. The menu is inspired by Mexican and Korean cuisine, but there are also some dishes that are truly Russian, such as their most popular dish, Forest Pancake. Thought up by Pavel and his team, this can't be found in any other Russian restaurant, and it encapsulates the essence of the nation's cuisine: generous, pure and delicious.

Follow them on
Instagram: @belki_uglevody

62

How to make it

SERVES 5

Ingredients
For the pancake batter:
250g (9oz) buttermilk
100g (3½oz) plain flour
1 egg
½ tbs sugar (optional)
pinch of salt
½ tsp baking powder
1½ tbs oil
melted butter, for brushing

For the fillings:
350g (12oz) potatoes
75ml (2½fl oz) milk
40g (1½oz) butter
salt & ground black pepper, to taste
250g (9oz) fresh chanterelle mushrooms, sliced
4 dried juniper berries, crushed
small handful of pink peppercorns, crushed
½ tbs gin
100g (3½oz) bacon, diced
1 tsp pine cone jam
splash of balsamic vinegar
small handful of crispy onions
small handful of pickled cucumbers, chopped
pinch of dill, chopped

small handful of spring onions, chopped
100g (3½oz) Greek yoghurt

Method
1. Bring a pan of salted water to the boil, add the potatoes, cook until tender, then drain.

2. In a pan, heat the milk and 25g (1oz) of the butter, until melted.

3. Mash the potatoes, slowly adding the milk, until smooth. Season to taste.

4. Fry the chanterelles in the remaining butter until soft, then add the juniper berries, peppercorns and gin. Transfer to a plate.

5. Fry the bacon with the jam and vinegar. Set aside.

6. For the pancakes, whisk together all ingredients except the oil and butter, until smooth.

7. Heat some oil in a medium frying pan over a medium heat, add some batter and cook on each side, until golden.

8. Transfer to a plate, brush with melted butter and keep warm while you make more pancakes.

9. Spoon the potato into the middle of each pancake, then

add chanterelles, bacon, crispy onions, cucumbers, dill, spring onions and yoghurt.

10. Wrap the pancake and fry on each side for 30 seconds. Serve.

SOUTH AFRICAN MQA

with truffle oil & fragrant tomato sauce

4ROOMED EKASI CULTURE, CAPE TOWN, SOUTH AFRICA

Scoring a spot in the South African version of *MasterChef* completely changed the course of Abigail Mbalo-Mokoena's life. Within months of appearing on the show, the former dental technician had left her career behind and in 2014 she launched her own food truck, 4Roomed eKasi Culture. Named after the typical four-roomed houses found in South Africa's old townships - and indeed the house Abigail grew up in - the truck is a celebration of local life. The dishes on offer sit in a category of their own: traditional township food elevated to fine-dining status. The truck was the perfect way to test out the concept, and after three years of satisfied customers with satisfied tummies, Abigail opened a restaurant in a four-roomed house in Khayelitsha, 30km (18½ miles) from Cape Town. These days the truck is only used for special events, but the traditional-meets-contemporary cuisine is available at the restaurant as a multi-course banquet.

Follow them on
Facebook: www.facebook.com/4RoomedeKasi

How to make it

🌿 SERVES 4

Ingredients
For the *mqa*:
200g (7oz) roasted butternut
    squash
50ml (2fl oz) vegetable stock
200ml (7fl oz) water
pinch of ground nutmeg
pinch of salt
100g (3¾oz) butter
200g (7oz) cornmeal or polenta
200g (7oz) seasonal
    mushrooms
drizzle of truffle-infused olive oil

For the tomato sauce:
200g (7oz) large, ripe tomatoes,
    quartered
1 medium pepper, quartered
1 large onion, quartered
2 garlic cloves, crushed
pinch of salt
2 tbs soft light brown sugar
100ml (3½fl oz) olive oil
handful of basil leaves,
    chopped
1 sprig of thyme

Method
1. For the *mqa*, put the squash in a large pan with the stock and water and bring to the boil.

2. Add nutmeg, salt and 50g (2oz) of the butter.

3. Slowly pour in the cornmeal while stirring briskly with a whisk. Cook for 30-45 minutes, until the grains become slightly translucent and the maize grains bind together. The cornmeal, when cooked, will give out a scent of freshly baked bread.

4. Meanwhile, make the tomato sauce. Preheat the oven to 200°C (400°F). Put the tomatoes, pepper, onion and garlic in a roasting pan, sprinkle with salt and roast for 15 minutes.

5. Transfer to a food processor, add the sugar, half of the olive oil, the basil and thyme and blitz until smooth.

6. Pour into a pan and add the remaining oil. Heat gently, stirring often.

7. In a frying pan, sauté the mushrooms in the remaining butter with a pinch of salt.

8. Drizzle the *mqa* with truffle oil, top with the mushrooms and serve with the tomato sauce.

ASIAN BACON BURGER

DIE WORS ROL, CAPE TOWN, SOUTH AFRICA

When Craig Cormack and Bertus Basson launched Die Wors Rol in 2011, neither was a stranger to the local culinary scene. Both chefs had long-running careers in fine dining, but the lighthearted nature of running a food truck appealed to the duo, so they put aside the caviar and set out to create the perfect gourmet hot dog. Basson has since left the partnership, opening various restaurants and appearing on gourmet TV shows. But the food truck remains unchanged and Cormack continues to feed hungry fans at festivals, special events and the occasional market. He admits that running a food truck isn't as romantic as people often think, and that the prep can be a killer, but once he's serving his creations straight to the public, he insists it doesn't feel like work at all.

How to make it

SERVES 4

Ingredients
1kg (2¼lb) rolled pork belly

For the banh mi marinade:
475ml (16fl oz) fish sauce
300g (11oz) sugar
150g (5oz) Thai yellow curry paste
120ml (4fl oz) lime juice
1 tsp ginger puree
1 tsp ground turmeric
3 garlic cloves, thinly sliced
2 lemongrass stalks, thinly sliced
1 Thai red chilli, thinly sliced
1 shallot, thinly sliced
handful kaffir lime leaves, finely
    diced (or 1 tbs lime juice)
3 sprigs Thai basil leaves, torn

For the curry aioli:
225g (8oz) mayonnaise
90g (3½oz) sugar
2 tbs fish sauce
2 tbs lime juice
1 tbs curry powder
1 tsp ginger juice
1 tsp sriracha chilli sauce
1 tsp ground turmeric

To serve:
4 sweet bread buns
165g (5½oz) green lettuce
75g (3oz) carrots, julienned
75g (3oz) daikon, julienned

Method
1. For the marinade, whisk the fish sauce and sugar in a large bowl until the sugar is dissolved.

2. Add the curry paste, whisk until combined. Add the remaining ingredients and mix well.

3. Rub most of the marinade all over the rolled pork belly and leave overnight. Keep some marinade for further glazing.

4. Preheat an oven to 120°C (250°F) or set up a smoker and cook the pork for 5 hours, then chill. When the belly is cooled, slice into desired-size patties.

5. For the aioli, whisk together all the ingredients until smooth. Set aside and chill.

6. Dip the patties in the remaining marinade to form a crust, then grill them on medium heat until heated through and sizzling.

7. Fill each bun with a patty, lettuce, carrots and daikon. Top with a dollop of curry aioli.

CHICKEN TIKKA

with slaw & naan

HANGRY CHEF, JOHANNESBURG, SOUTH AFRICA

Chef Dalmain Samuel started his food truck, originally named Chilli Chef, in September 2016. A few months later, Dalmain's wife Lynelle quit her corporate job to join the business; since then the food truck has flourished, and was recently rebranded 'Hangry Chef'. The Durban couple are of Indian descent, but the food they serve is not purely Indian. When they were growing up, Lynelle explains, their parents cooked both Indian and Western dishes, but even the Western dishes had a bit of Indian flavour. 'You'd still use a lot of Indian spices, like the garam masala or curry powders,' Lynelle says. Dalmain brings this combination of influences to the Hangry Chef's menu, where chicken burgers and beef stew sing with spices. Find the truck at the Friday Hoods Market in Sandton, or at the Standard Bank headquarters in downtown Jo'burg, as well as at events and private functions.

Follow them on
Instagram: @hangrychefft
Facebook: www.facebook.com/HangryChefFT

How to make it

SERVES 4

Ingredients
4 tbs curry powder
4 tbs vegetable oil
2 tbs garlic puree
2 tbs red food colouring (optional)
pinch of salt
4 free-range chicken breasts
4 naans

For the slaw:
½ head of red cabbage, finely sliced
2 carrots, grated
4 tbs mayo
salt, to taste

For the sauce:
100ml (3½fl oz) thick natural yoghurt
1 tsp mint sauce
pinch of salt

Method
1. First, prepare the chicken. Combine the curry powder, oil, garlic, optional food colouring and salt in a large, shallow dish, then add the chicken and turn to coat in the marinade. Cover and leave in the fridge for 24 hours.

2. Heat a large frying pan over medium-high heat, add the chicken and cook for 20–25 minutes, flipping the chicken after 10–12 minutes, until cooked through. Set aside to rest for 10 minutes.

3. Mix together all the slaw ingredients.

4. Mix together all the sauce ingredients.

5. Place a line of the slaw on each naan.

6. Cut the chicken into pieces and place on the slaw.

7. Drizzle the sauce over the chicken to finish.

69

'Someone can eat
my *chakalaka* today,
tomorrow, every day.
I never change – it's the
same thing every day.'
Tselane 'Johanna' Ditsele,
owner

CHAKALAKA RELISH

TSELANE'S KITCHEN, JOHANNESBURG, SOUTH AFRICA

Tselane 'Johanna' Ditsele spent many years cooking and cleaning in a private home before deciding to find a new career. After experimenting with several locations around Midrand, a far-northern suburb with dozens of office complexes, Johanna settled on a spot in 16th Road. During lunch, a stream of cars pulls up to buy containers bursting with food. Like many other trailers set up by the roadside for Jo'burg's weekday lunch rush, Tselane's Kitchen serves traditional South African food: fat cake (fried dough balls) stuffed with curried mince; steak, roast chicken or beef stew with pap (maize meal porridge) and gravy; and various side dishes, such as beetroot salad, *morogo* (African spinach), and *chakalaka*. The latter, which originated in townships, is a hot and spicy relish made with vegetables, canned beans and chillies/spices. Johanna's *chakalaka* is simple, with just five ingredients, but she says it's what keeps her customers coming back.

Where are they now?
16th Rd, Jo'burg, across from the Hyundai Midrand car dealership.

How to make it

🌿 SERVES 4

(AS A SIDE DISH)

Ingredients
3 tsp vegetable oil
½ large onion, finely chopped
6 carrots, finely chopped
1 green pepper, finely chopped
5 green chillies (medium heat), chopped
1 x 400g (14oz) can baked beans
salt, to taste

Method
1. Put the oil in a large pan and place over medium heat.

2. Once hot, add the onion and fry for about 7 minutes, until soft but not translucent.

3. Add the carrots, pepper and chillies, stir to combine, then cook for 5 minutes.

4. Add the baked beans and simmer for 5 minutes. Add salt to taste.

5. Serve at room temperature or cold. *Chakalaka* thickens the longer it sits.

'Mama Rocks is pioneering the Nairobi street food scene with an Afro-cool food truck like no other. We want everybody to know how great African food is!'
Samantha & Natalie Mwedekel, co-founders

PAW PAW POW BURGER

MAMA ROCKS GOURMET BURGER, NAIROBI, KENYA

Mama Rocks is without doubt Nairobi's best-loved food truck. Started by two Kenyan-Nigerian sisters, Samantha and Natalie, it has given the 'Gourmet Burger' an authentic, African twist. Pioneering the food truck scene wasn't easy, though, as Nairobi was on the cusp of regulating the innovative sector, but today their truck roams between the buzzing Alchemist Bar and music festivals, where it draws a young, urban crowd. It may be a modest-sized truck, but the flavours are fresh and bold. Each burger represents a different part of Africa - the signature dish being the Paw Paw Pow Burger, named after the sisters' first trip to Nigeria and their first taste of the succulent, sweet fruit. The Kenya-themed Mango Masai Mama Burger - packed with chilli mango mayonnaise, Cheddar cheese and roasted pepper - is also a favourite. The sisters hope their eclectic menu will educate and inspire people to learn more about African cuisine.

Follow them on
Instagram: @mamarocksbgk
Facebook: www.facebook.com/mamarocksburgers

How to make it

SERVES 4

Ingredients
725g (1lb 10oz) coarsely minced beef (chuck, rib-eye or topside)
4 tbs sunflower oil
8 beef or pork bacon rashers
200g (7oz) halloumi cheese, sliced
4 brioche buns, split in half
4 tbs mayonnaise
8 gem lettuce leaves
1 large red onion, thinly sliced into rings

For the paw paw barbecue sauce:
1 ripe paw paw, peeled & coarsely chopped
1 small red onion, diced
225g (8oz) brown sugar
225g (8oz) ketchup
350ml (12fl oz) apple cider vinegar
50g (2oz) hot sauce
1 tsp cayenne pepper

Method
1. Combine all the barbecue sauce ingredients into a large pan and simmer on a medium heat for about 30 minutes, stirring regularly. Remove from the heat, leave to cool, then blend and set aside.

2. Make your beef patties by weighing 180g (6½oz) of mince for each, forming balls and flattening these into discs by hand.

3. Place a frying pan over a medium-high heat. Brush the burger patties with a little of the oil, then cook for approximately 3 minutes on each side.

4. Spoon 1½ tsp of the barbecue sauce on to one side of the burger patty and let it cook for about 2 minutes, then repeat on the other side of the patty until fully cooked (the juices run clear).

5. Meanwhile, fry the bacon and halloumi in a separate pan in a little oil until both are golden brown.

6. To assemble: spread each bun with mayonnaise, 2 gem lettuce leaves, beef patty, halloumi, bacon, onion rings, bun crown.

'I am sure that we can meet the challenges we face; we have to, because we have to serve as an example for others in our community.'
Mariam Chaar, founder

LEBANESE MSAKHAN

SOUFRA, BEIRUT, LEBANON

The cooks behind Soufra haven't had it easy. As women from the Burj el-Barajneh Palestinian refugee camp in Beirut, they've faced grinding poverty and legal restrictions on education and job prospects since the camp's founding in 1948. Founded by Mariam Chaar, Soufra has a weekly stand at a farmers market, where the food truck sells its signature dishes, including a transcendent version of the Palestinian national dish *msakhan*. Chaar started Soufra, which means 'table of plenty', in 2013 to create opportunities for members of her community most in need of jobs; since then over 40 women have benefitted from the programme and in 2017, Susan Sarandon produced a documentary about Chaar's uphill battle to purchase and outfit the truck. Fuelled by Palestinian delicacies, the women's energy seems boundless.

Follow them on
Facebook: www.facebook.com/soufralebanon

How to make it

SERVES 4

(AS A SNACK)

Ingredients

1 tbs extra virgin olive oil, plus extra for brushing
1 large onion, sliced
25g (1oz) sumac
¼ tsp ground cinnamon
¼ tsp ground cardamom
¼ tsp ground cloves
pinch of saffron
¼ tsp allspice
salt, to taste
freshly ground black pepper
200g (7oz) roasted chicken leg meat, skin discarded, meat stripped from the bone and shredded
25g (1oz) almonds or pine nuts, toasted
markouk bread or 4 flour tortillas

Method

1. Heat 1 tbs of the oil in a large pan over medium heat.

2. Add the onion and cook, stirring occasionally, for 10 minutes.

3. Add the spices, salt and pepper and stir to combine.

4. Add the shredded chicken and nuts and stir well.

5. Allow the chicken mixture to cool. Preheat the oven to 150°C (300°F).

6. Meanwhile, cut the *markouk* or tortilla bread into 8 large triangles.

7. Put a spoonful of the chicken mixture in the middle of each triangle, then fold two sides in and roll it up into a cigar shape.

8. Brush the remaining oil all over the *msakhan* and arrange on baking sheets.

9. Bake for 10 minutes, or until crispy. Serve immediately.

'Bombay is an emotion. Bombay Food Truck only amplifies what I feel for the city.'
Ashish Sajnani, founder

KEEMA PAV

with pickled beetroot

BOMBAY FOOD TRUCK, MUMBAI, INDIA

Launched in September 2015, Bombay Food Truck is one of India's finest street food sellers, with a fleet of three sizzling-red trucks. Inspired by the founder Ashish Sajnani's travels and a first brush with food trucks in Europe as a student and then in the USA, Bombay Food Truck hopes to marry the local flavours of Mumbai with the atmospheric street food scene. Some of the most popular delicacies on the menu include salads, hot dogs, burgers and *pav bhaji* (a Mumbai-style white bun stuffed with fillings). Located permanently at One BKC, the truck can also cater for breakfasts, lunches and dinners at private weddings, private parties, corporate events and festivals.

Follow them on
Instagram: @bombayfoodtruck

How to make it

SERVES 1

Ingredients
1 multigrain *kadak pav*
  (large crusty roll)
1 egg
pinch of microgreens, to garnish
25g (1oz) pickled beetroot,
  to serve
minty raita, to serve

For the chicken keema masala:
2 tsp vegetable oil
1 tsp finely chopped onion
1 tsp finely chopped garlic
1 tsp finely chopped celery
75g (3oz) minced chicken
1 tbs red wine
2 tsp tomato puree
2 tsp harissa paste
2 tsp chicken stock
½ tsp salt
½ tsp ground black pepper
½ tsp dried thyme
1 tsp chopped coriander leaves

Method
1. First, to make the chicken keema masala, heat the oil in a pan over medium heat.

2. Add the onion, garlic and celery and sauté for 10 minutes, until softened.

3. Add the chicken and cook, stirring, for 5 minutes, then add all the remaining ingredients apart from the coriander.

4. Cook until all the stock has been absorbed, then stir in the coriander.

5. Preheat the oven to 180°C (350°F).

6. Cut off the top and remove the inside of the *kadak pav*, then put it on a baking tray.

7. Spoon the chicken keema masala into the cored-out *kadak pav* and use a spoon to make a dip in the mixture.

8. Break an egg in the dip and bake for about 10 minutes, until the egg is cooked.

9. Garnish with microgreens and serve with pickled beetroot and minty raita on the side.

PITAYA BOWL

PRINCESS KITCHEN, HONG KONG, CHINA

The *pitaya*, aka 'dragon fruit', is aptly named - egg-shaped, with a scaly, fuchsia skin, looking like something laid by a mythological fire-breathing creature. At Princess Kitchen, the wild-looking fruit is the star of their signature dish: the pitaya bowl. Frozen dragon fruit is blended to a sorbet-like consistency and topped with healthy goodies - granola, bananas, strawberries, blueberries, coconut shavings and goji berries. The robin's-egg blue truck, hand-painted by owner Angela Huang with images of 'princesses' from all walks of life, opened in 2016 as part of an official food truck scheme in a city relatively unfamiliar with the concept. But Huang, a Stanford graduate, knew about food trucks' popularity overseas - she did her pre-opening research by visiting California food trucks, even taking orders in one to gain experience. Today, Princess Kitchen sets up shop all over town: Hong Kong Disneyland, charity events, and - appropriately - the annual dragon boat races.

**Follow them on
Instagram:** @princesskitchenhk

How to make it

🍃 SERVES 3–4

Ingredients
200g (7oz) pink dragon fruit, chopped & frozen
200g (7oz) white dragon fruit, chopped & frozen
200g (7oz) banana, chopped & frozen

For the toppings:
4 tbs granola
12 strawberries, hulled & quartered
handful of blueberries
2 tbs goji berries
1 tbs coconut sha[vings]
1 tbs chia seeds
2 tbs honey

Method
1. Place the frozen dragon fruit flesh and banana in a blender and blend until sorbet-like in consistency.

2. Pour into cups or bowls and divide the toppings evenly between the portions.

'The best part of working on the truck is being able to meet travellers from all over the world. Everyone tells us how Instagrammable and *kawaii* we are!'
Mimi Kojima, co-owner

HAWAIIAN GARLIC SHRIMP

with rice & okinawan vegetables

KOURI SHRIMP, KOURI ISLAND, JAPAN

Blown away by Kouri Island's ocean views, Yumiko Omine and Mimi Kojima moved here from Tokyo to open Kouri Shrimp in 2014. 'It was love at first sight,' Mimi says. Observing the climate's similarity to Oahu Island, they decided on Hawaiian-inspired shrimp served with rice and a side of Okinawan vegetables as their speciality. 'We thought the dish could be familiar, but new,' Mimi adds. The pink and blue-green truck sits in a parking lot steps from the beach where it meets Kouri Bridge, a 2km connection that leads to the mainland. Kouri Shrimp's menu includes four kinds of garlic shrimp, thinly sliced French fries and a side of Onaha beef, but the original garlic shrimp plate remains king of the truck. Pairing their juicy, seasoned crustaceans with a canned Hawaiian Sun or a cold beer, visitors can enjoy their meal with the crystal waters crashing at their feet.

**Follow them on
Instagram:** @kourishrimp

How to make it

SERVES 1

Ingredients

7–8 pieces of shrimp
1 tbs flour
3 tbs olive oil
3 tbs crushed garlic
1 tbs vinegar
1–2 tbs rock salt
pinch of ground black pepper
1 tbs mixed herbs
125g (4¼oz) cooked rice
1 tbs soy sauce

For the accompaniments (optional)

thinly sliced red onion
1 slice of goya (sometimes called Okinawan bitter melon)
1 slice of lemon
1 slice of corn on the cob
Okinawan sweet potato chips

Method

1. Prepare the shrimp by washing them and butterflying each one with a sharp knife. Leave the shrimp in cold water until ready to cook, then drain well, so the shrimp are as dry as possible.

2. Dredge the d[...] through a thin la[...]

3. Heat the olive [...] the garlic in a large wok or skillet over medium heat, then add the shrimp and fry for 1–2 minutes until pink and slightly crispy.

4. Add the vinegar, salt, pepper, herbs and remaining garlic and toss to combine.

5. Serve the rice on to a plate, sprinkle with soy sauce and top with the shrimp and all the seasonings in the pan.

6. Serve with your choice of accompaniments.

DETOX AÇAI BOWL

AÇAI CORNER, PERTH, AUSTRALIA

This energising food truck was founded in 2016 on the beaches of Perth, Australia, but the real story started when Maddie and Andrew Russell quit their jobs to travel slowly through South America. After spending a month in Cuba with very little fresh fruit or vegetables, they sat down at a cafe in Copacabana in Rio de Janeiro and had a freshly squeezed orange juice and a bowl of açai. They had never had this food before, didn't know how to pronounce it or what it really was, but it was the first time in so long that they felt nourished. And so the two scrapped their plans to head south and instead flew into the Amazon rainforest. There they scaled açai palm trees, shared meals, stories and laughter with the harvesters, traversed the Amazon River, embraced the chaotic açai markets before dawn, toured the factories where açai is produced and ate (a lot of) the powerful berry. Though tricky to pronounce ('ah-sigh-ee') the berry is hailed as one of the most antioxidant rich foods on the planet. Açai Corner has an extensive range of natural açai bowls, but the Detox Açai Bowl is still their best seller.

Follow them on
Instagram: www.instagram.com/theacaicorner

How to make it

🌿 **SERVES 4**

Ingredients
For the base:
2 packs of natural, unsweetened açai
½ banana
1 handful of mango chunks
1 cup of coconut water

For the topping:
½ cup granola (ideally homemade)
1 tbs of dry coconut
2 tsp cacao nibs
1 tsp chia seeds
½ banana
3 strawberries
5 blueberries
1 tbs of passion fruit

Method
1. Put the açai, banana, mango and coconut water into a blender.

2. Blend until smooth in consistency – watch it doesn't go too far as you want to retain a thick creamy, not watery, consistency. Hint: If the açai is too hard when you remove it from the freezer, either leave out at room temp for 10 minutes or run it under some water to thaw.

3. Spoon the açai blitz into a bowl of your choosing.

4. Spoon the granola, coconut, cacao nibs and chia seeds on top of the açai base.

5. Arrange the fruits to your liking (we like banana and strawberry alternating around the outside and then blueberries and passionfruit towards the centre). But there are no rules! Have fun with the topping and get creative.

CAROLINA SMOKED PULLED PORK SANDWICH

with slaw, pickles & fries

SNEAKY PICKLE, ADELAIDE, AUSTRALIA

Sneaky Pickle was one of the first food trucks in Adelaide in 2012 and now has a cult following. Inspired by the towering Jewish pastrami sandwiches they'd encountered in New York City, chefs Jeff and Amanda Griffiths quit their restaurant jobs and bought a van. Adelaideans took a while to warm to the rather 'un-Australian' formula of hot meat in a cold sandwich, but after a year Sneaky Pickle went from selling 30 lunchtime sandwiches to 80, then 100, then 150… Heading back to the US every year for inspiration, Jeff and Amanda have eaten their way across the South, dipping into Texan, Mexican, cowboy and 'soul food' influences. They soon expanded their menu to include Carolina pulled pork and BBQ beef brisket sandwiches; big-selling, big-hearted meals. And now there's a Sneaky Pickle restaurant too!

Follow them on
Facebook www.facebook.com/adelaidesownsneakypickle

How to make it

SERVES 4

Ingredients
1 pork butt or shoulder,
    about 2½kg (5½lb)
soft white rolls
French fries, to serve
deep-fried pickles, to serve

For the spice rub:
120g (4oz) dark brown sugar
60g (2oz) paprika
25g (1oz) ground black pepper
25g (1oz) salt
25g (1oz) garlic powder
½ tsp chilli powder

For the Carolina sauce:
125ml (4fl oz) cider vinegar
60g (2oz) soft light brown sugar
60ml (2fl oz) pickle juice

For the slaw:
125g (5oz) red cabbage
125g (5oz) white cabbage
1 small carrot
handful of flat parsley leaves
120g (4oz) mayonnaise
½ tbs American mustard
pinch of ground black pepper

Method
1. Mix the spice rub ingredients together in a large bowl. Thoroughly rub the mixture into the pork and allow to stand for at least 1 hour.

2. Preheat oven to 120°C (250°F) or set up a smoker, and cook the pork for around 3 hours, until tender. For smokers, aromatic cherrywood is preferred.

3. Pull the cooked meat from the bone (chop if needed) and place in a deep tray.

4. Combine the sauce ingredients and pour over the pork.

5. For the slaw, core the cabbages and shred the leaves into long, thin strips. Grate the carrot and coarsely chop the parsley, then combine with the cabbage. Stir in mayonnaise and mustard and add pepper to taste. For a less-sweet result, use less carrot.

6. To serve, scoop pork into halved rolls, top with slaw and cap with the roll lid. Serve with a side of French fries and deep-fried pickles.

THE BAHH

(lamb souvlaki)

GREEK STREET FOOD, MELBOURNE, AUSTRALIA

The man behind Melbourne's first Greek food truck has an impeccable culinary pedigree: George Karanikos used to run the critically acclaimed Pireaus Blues on Fitzroy's Brunswick St, until its closure in 2016. After a bit of soul-searching, George woke his wife Flora at 6am to tell her his idea: to bring authentic Greek street food to Melbourne. Flora thought he was mad. Watching him obsessively research food trucks, though, she realised he was serious. His son James was next to get the wake-up call, the idea this time to name all the meals after animal sounds: the Bahh, the Cluck, the Oink. Fast-forward a few years and George's souvlakis are in high demand - his 'souva mobile' (with murals by James) gets an almighty reception whenever any Greeks see it. He's also opened a permanent site in Thornbury, with Flora overseeing operations and daughter Karlita in the kitchen and front of house.

Follow them on
Instagram: @greekstreetfood
Twitter: @gsfoodau

How to make it

SERVES 6

Ingredients
For the tzatziki:
500g (1lb) thick, natural Greek yoghurt (strained in muslin for 2 hours)
40g (1½oz) Lebanese cucumbers, grated into muslin and squeezed to remove excess liquid
½ garlic clove, crushed
½ tbs olive oil
salt, to taste

For the lamb:
500g (1lb) lamb fillet
1 tsp sea salt
½ tsp crushed garlic
½ tbs Greek oregano
1 tbs olive oil, plus extra for brushing
pinch of cracked black pepper

To serve:
6 small pittas, warmed
1-2 tomatoes, sliced
1 red onion, finely sliced
1-2 potatoes, cut into chips and deep-fried in olive oil
salt, to taste
oregano, to taste

Method
1. Combine all the tzatziki ingredients in a bowl and set aside.

2. Trim any sinew from the lamb fillet, then dice into 2cm (¾in) pieces.

3. In a bowl, stir the lamb with the salt, garlic, oregano, oil and pepper until well mixed.

4. Thread the pieces of lamb on to skewers and leave to marinate for at least 1 hour if possible.

5. Preheat a grill, barbecue or griddle plan and cook the lamb for 10–12 minutes, turning and brushing with olive oil. Remove the lamb from the skewers and set aside.

6. To assemble each wrap, take a warm pitta and spread with about 2 tbs tzatziki. Add a few slices of tomato, some onion, potato chips, salt, oregano and the lamb. Roll up and enjoy.

MR CHICKEN BURGER

MR BURGER, MELBOURNE (ALSO HOBART & BRISBANE), AUSTRALIA

Mr Burger is the result of a 2012 trip to the USA by founders Daragh Kan and Myles Munro. They brought the idea home, and their orange Mr Burger trucks were some of the first food trucks to hit Melbourne's streets. There's an element of fun when it comes to the concept but, according to Kan, things don't always go to plan. 'One idea was that we would give people free burgers for life if they changed their last name to Burger, but a few days later we got a letter from the Victorian Attorney General saying they won't allow any name changes.' So no one became Mr or Mrs Burger, but it did make the news. They turned an old garage into Welcome to Thornbury, a food truck park with a buzzing bar and events centre and a rotating roster of food trucks. Permanent Mr Burger restaurants have opened around Melbourne too.

Follow them on
Instagram: @mrburgertruck
Facebook: @mrburgertruck

How to make it

SERVES 2

Ingredients
2 x 130–150g (4½–5oz) boneless, skinless chicken thighs (brined is best)
vegetable oil, for deep-frying
salt, to taste
2 burger buns
1 tbs butter
8 tbs ranch dressing
shredded lettuce, to serve
6 pickle slices

For the Mr Chicken Flour
60g (2½oz) plain flour
15g (½oz) tapioca flour
15g (½oz) potato flour
15g (½oz) cornflour
1 tbs chicken salt

Method
1. Combine all the ingredients for the Mr Chicken Flour and tip some into a shallow dish.

2. Add the chicken thighs and turn to coat thoroughly. Cover and refrigerate for at least 6 hours.

3. Coat the chicken in flour again.

4. Heat the oil in a large, heavy pan or deep-fryer to 190°C (375°F).

5. Add the thighs and fry for 5 minutes, until golden and crispy.

6. Remove from the fryer, shake off excess oil and test the temperature of the chicken with a food thermometer. It needs to read at least 76°C (169°F). If not, fry the chicken for longer.

7. Place the chicken on a resting tray and season with salt. Cut the buns in half, toast, then spread with butter.

8. Spread 2 tbs of ranch dressing on both bun halves, then put some lettuce on the bottom bun, followed by the chicken, pickles and the top bun.

TUSCAN BEEF RAGU

with potato gnocchi

PASTA FACE, MELBOURNE, AUSTRALIA

Parents from Calabria and Asiago, trained by superchef Guy Grossi… all the ingredients were there, it just took Daniel D'Agostino's wife to realise he should run Melbourne's first pasta food truck. Having burned himself out in the restaurant industry, Daniel had taken a job in a printing company, but in 2015 he was still making homemade pasta for family and friends and thought he would give it a go. Starting out at Yarraville Gardens, he met people like George Karanikos from Greek Street Food (p86), who gave him helpful advice. After some experimentation, he has convinced Melburnians to turn their 'I can do that at home' attitude around, and now there are queues for his authentic, restaurant-quality Italian fare. The secret is the detail: his dad prepares the chilli in a special way, the gnocchi is handmade, the ragu is simmered for 6 hours and there are Parmesan and truffle chips.

Follow them on
Instagram: @pastafacetruck
Facebook: www.facebook.com/pastafacetruck

How to make it

SERVES 2

Ingredients
500g (18oz) beef (shin/shank), trimmed into 2.5cm (1in) pieces
1 large bunch of fresh basil (leaves picked, washed & spun-dried)
25ml (1fl oz) vegetable oil
25ml (1fl oz) olive oil
1 onion, diced
1 garlic clove, finely chopped
salt, to taste
ground white pepper, to taste
nutmeg, to taste
1 bay leaf
70g (2½oz) tomato paste
100ml (3½fl oz) red cooking wine
500g (18oz) passata
1L (1¾ pints) water
300g (10½oz) homemade potato gnocchi, to serve

Method
1. Preheat the oven to 200–220°C (400–425°F).

2. Season the beef on a large tray with salt and pepper. Roast for about 40 minutes, until the meat is brown. Remove from the oven and cover.

3. Puree the basil with the vegetable oil to make a paste.

4. Put the olive oil in a very large, heavy pan over a medium heat. Add the onion and garlic and sauté for 10–15 minutes, until translucent. Season with salt, white pepper and nutmeg.

5. Add the basil puree and the bay leaf. Stir in the tomato paste, allowing it to stick and cook on the base of the pan.

6. Pour in the wine, stirring continually, and leave to reduce for a few minutes.

7. Add the passata and water. Bring to the boil, then reduce to low heat and add the beef and its juices.

8. Simmer on low heat for 4–6 hours, stirring regularly, until the meat is falling apart.

9. Remove the bay leaves and serve with potato gnocchi.

THE FONZ TOASTIE

TOASTA, MELBOURNE, AUSTRALIA

When Rebecca Feingold first saw the utility truck that was to become Toasta, it was covered in red dust from the Northern Territory. It was cleaned up, built up and launched as Melbourne's only toasted sandwich truck in 2014. When deciding between the Mack Daddy, with pulled pork and mac 'n' cheese, and the Shane, with chicken schnitzel, it's hard to believe Rebecca studied nutrition. But for the owner whose dad used to make jaffles and Milo milkshakes every Saturday morning, it's about bringing people together. 'I've always loved cooking for people and sharing food', she says. Toasta makes the rounds at festivals, markets and events, and in 2016 Toasta opened a permanent store in West Melbourne. Whether served with tomato bisque in winter or deep-fried potato the morning after a big night, there's a taste of nostalgia with Toasta.

Follow them on
Instagram: @toastafoodtruck
Facebook: www.facebook.com/toastafoodtruck

How to make it

SERVES 1

Ingredients
2 streaky bacon rashers
6 walnut halves, roughly chopped
1 tbs duck fat
115g (4oz) fontina cheese, grated
2 thick slices of organic sourdough bread
1 tsp white truffle oil
1 small handful of rocket

Method

1. Preheat a sandwich press, or heat a cast-iron press for 15 minutes on a cast-iron pan, hot plate or barbecue.

2. Heat a heavy pan, hot plate or flat-top barbecue and cook the bacon rashers, flipping to brown both sides.

3. Place the walnuts in an ungreased pan over medium heat, stirring often until golden. Remove from the heat.

4. Spread the duck fat on the outside of both pieces of bread.

5. With the duck fat side down, place half the grated cheese on one piece of bread, followed by the walnuts and bacon rashers.

6. Evenly drizzle the truffle oil over the top, then finish with the remaining cheese. Place the second piece of bread on top, duck fat side up.

7. Place the toastie in the sandwich press. If using a cast-iron press, place it on a non-stick pan, hot plate or flat-top barbecue over medium heat, and place the cast-iron press on top, applying some pressure.

8. Cook the toastie for 3–4 minutes on each side, until both are golden and the cheese is melted.

9. Open the toastie and place the rocket inside and cook for a further 30 seconds to allow the rocket to wilt.

10. Remove the toastie, cut in half and serve.

BUTTER PANEER MASALA

YO INDIA, MELBOURNE, AUSTRALIA

Meet the Gomes family. Originally from Calcutta but calling Melbourne home, they've also lived in Europe, where they had a restaurant in Romania. In 2014 they started Big Cook Little Cook, later changing the name to Yo India and incorporating flavour combinations from their travels. 'It's not your typical Indian menu,' says Conan, one of the sons in the family business. Indeed, their biggest sellers are a tandoori platter that comes with hummus and beef tacos with a south-Indian spin. Conan's father is a chef and has the final say on traditional recipes passed down from his own father. At the time of writing, the Gomes family is hunting for a location, but food truck freedom has its own appeal. 'We get to explore different parts of Melbourne along with their communities,' says Conan. 'We still find a lot of people who haven't tried Indian food or had a bad experience in a restaurant, but once they try it with us they are pleasantly surprised.'

Follow them on
Instagram: @yoindia.au
Facebook: facebook.com/yoindia.au

How to make it

🌿 SERVES 2

Ingredients
100g (3¾oz) ghee or butter
500g (1¼lb) paneer cubes
225g (8oz) onion paste
1 tsp ginger & garlic paste
1½ tsp chilli powder
2 tsp garam masala
2 tsp sugar
salt, to taste
115g (4oz) tomato puree
150ml (¼ pint) water
3 tbs double cream
naan or pilau rice, to serve
1 tsp dried fenugreek leaves,
   to garnish

Method
1. Heat half the ghee or butter in a pan and add the paneer. Fry, shaking to toss, until golden brown all over. Remove from the heat and set aside.

2. Heat the remaining ghee or butter in the same pan, then add the onion paste, and ginger and garlic paste. Mix well and cook for 5 minutes on a medium heat.

3. Add the chilli powder, garam masala, sugar, salt and tomato puree. Mix well and cook for 5 minutes.

4. Add the paneer and water, mix well and simmer for 5 minutes.

5. Add the cream and simmer for another 2 minutes.

6. Serve hot with naan or pilau rice, garnished with fenugreek leaves.

VEGETARIAN NACHOS

CANTINA MOVIL, SYDNEY, AUSTRALIA

Stephanie Waco and Rode Vella hail from Sydney's Northern Beaches, where they established InSitu, one of the first bar-restaurants in the area. After eight years, though, they got sick of working 'between four walls' and wanted to get out to where the fun was happening - big festivals and sporting events - so in 2012 they came up with Sydney's first food truck: Cantina Movil. Working with former InSitu chef Simon Livingston they developed a menu that could be prepped ahead, assembled quickly on board and eaten standing up. They wanted flexible dishes that would allow a broad range to be built around a small number of core elements, so Mexican food was the natural choice. One of these signature components is pinto beans, which appear in almost all their dishes, including these vegetarian nachos.

Follow them on
Instagram: @cantinamovil
Twitter: @cantina_movil

How to make it

🌿 SERVES 4

Ingredients
200g (7oz) dried pinto beans
½ tsp dried oregano
1 bay leaf
1 tbs olive oil
1 brown onion, finely sliced
1 fresh red chilli, seeds removed, finely sliced
2 garlic cloves, crushed
1½ tsp smoked paprika
1 tsp ground coriander
1½ tsp ground cumin
400g (14oz) can chopped tomatoes
1 tbs fresh oregano leaves, chopped
pinch of salt
pinch of ground black pepper

To serve (per person):
2 handfuls of corn chips
1 tbs *queso fresco* (cheese)
2 tbs mayonnaise
¾ tbs chipotle peppers, chopped
4 tbs guacamole
1 sprig of coriander leaves

Method
1. Soak the beans overnight. Then drain and rinse the beans, transfer to a large pan and cover with fresh water. Bring to the boil, then drain and rinse again.

2. Return the beans to the pan and cover with fresh cold water to cover by 1cm (½in). Add the dried oregano and bay leaf and simmer for 25–35 minutes.

3. Heat the oil in another large pan. Add the onion and chilli and cook, stirring, for about 10 minutes.

4. Meanwhile, blend the chipotle peppers and mayonnaise in a bowl until smooth. Set aside.

5. Add the garlic and dried spices to the pan, cook for 1 minute, then add the chopped tomatoes and fresh oregano and season, then simmer for 5 minutes.

6. When the beans are cooked, drain, reserving 5 tbs water. Add the beans and water to the tomato mixture. Bring back to the boil.

7. Create a bed of corn chips in a dish per person. Scoop on two serving spoons of pinto beans and sprinkle with grated *queso fresco*. Streak on chipotle sauce and guacamole in the centre and finish with fresh coriander leaves.

CURRYWURST

VOLKSWURST, SYDNEY, AUSTRALIA

Pascal Maier and Beau Avedissian have a passion for two things - cars and food - and decided after finishing high school to combine their loves. Having pimped the roof of a 40-year-old Kombi van so it opens like a jack-in-the-box, they installed a grill and speakers for 'volksmusik' and gave the whole thing a killer paint job. And so, in 2017, Volkswurst was born. This standout truck is no ordinary sausage sizzler. The pair are very serious about their wurst. Instead of serving Australian sausages, made from waste meat, fat and fillers wrapped in synthetic casings, the Volkswursters have their sausages specially made using just meat, natural casings and spices imported from Germany. They also make their own sauerkraut and sauces. As anyone who's been to Berlin knows, currywurst is an obsession there, and Pascal and Beau are dedicated to perfecting the sweet, peppery and piquant sauce that makes currywurst so special.

**Follow them on
Instagram: @Volkswurst**

How to make it

SERVES 5

Ingredients

5 Bockwurst or Knackwurst sausages
olive oil
3 bird's-eye chillies (more or less to taste)
400g (14oz) diced tomatoes
2 tbs honey
2 tbs red wine vinegar
1½ tbs vegetable stock
1 tbs Worcestershire sauce
3 tbs Sri Lankan curry powder, plus extra to garnish
1 tsp paprika
4 squirts of Tabasco sauce
bread rolls or chips, to serve

Method

1. The most important part of the recipe is the sausage. For this recipe that's a Knackwurst or a Bockwurst. A Knackwurst is a plump sausage from northern Germany smoked over natural hardwood – a bit like a frankfurter. A Bockwurst is made of veal and pork, erring on the veal side, and sometimes seasoned with chives or parsley. So find a very good German butcher, get your wurst, and fry them in plenty of oil in a frying pan until crispy all over.

2. In a separate pan, fry the chillies in a splash of oil.

3. Add the tomatoes, honey, red wine vinegar, stock, Worcestershire sauce, curry powder, paprika and Tabasco sauce and stir to combine.

4. Bring to the boil while stirring, then take off the heat and blend with a stick blender.

5. Slice up the sausages and drizzle the sauce on top, then garnish with a little extra curry powder. Serve with a bread roll or hot chips.

BRAISED EMU

with damper

CLINTO'S KUPMURRI, GOLD COAST, AUSTRALIA

When it launched in 2017, Clinto's Kupmurri was Australia's first Aboriginal-owned food truck with a focus on traditional cooking using native ingredients and promoting good health and Aboriginal culture. Based on the Gold Coast in a competitive market, owner and chef Clinton Schultz of the Gamilaraay people found his menu popular with a niche group of adventurous foodies and within the Aboriginal and Torres Strait Islander community. The 'kupmurri' is a traditional method of cooking a feast in an earth oven. Dishes with kangaroo, emu and crocodile are served alongside baked damper and salad with saltbush, samphire and warrigal greens. The truck itself was designed by an artist in the family who used the ochre and sand colours to reflect the Outback landscape. Recently handed over to new head chef Kieron Anderson, Clinto's now also serves Sobah, an alcoholic craft beer - the perfect accompaniment to authentic 'bush tucker'.

Follow them on
Instagram: @clintoskupmurri

How to make it

SERVES 4

Ingredients
1 tbs dried saltbush
1 tbs dried pepperberry
225g (8oz) plain flour
1kg (2¼lb) emu flank or rump (or lamb as a substitute)
2 tbs olive oil
750ml (1¼ pints) red wine
1 garlic clove, roughly chopped
1 onion, diced
2 long red chillies, seeded & finely chopped
2 x 400g (14oz) cans chopped tomatoes
½ bunch rosemary, finely chopped
½ bunch thyme, finely chopped
½ bunch fresh saltbush or parsley, finely chopped

For the damper:
500g (4½ cups) self-raising flour
good pinch of salt
75g (3oz) unsalted butter
200ml (7fl oz) lukewarm water

Method

1. Place half the saltbush and half the pepperberry in a plastic bag with the flour. Add the emu and toss until well coated.

2. Heat a large casserole or pan, add the oil and, when hot, add the emu and brown all over. Remove the emu from the pan and set aside.

3. Deglaze the pan with 120ml (4fl oz) of the wine.

4. Add the garlic, onion, saltbush, remaining pepperberry and chilli and cook for 10–15 minutes, until the onions are translucent.

5. Add the tomatoes, remaining wine, rosemary and thyme and bring to a simmer.

6. If you have one, transfer everything to a slow cooker or just leave in the casserole and cook on slow/low for at least 4 hours, preferably 6 hours.

7. Meanwhile, make the damper. Preheat the oven to 180°C (350°F).

8. Combine the flour and salt in a bowl, then rub in the butter until it resembles breadcrumbs.

9. Add water and mix until it just comes together (add a little extra water or flour as required).

10. Knead for 2 minutes, then divide into four, roll into hot dog bun shapes and place on a floured baking sheet.

11. Bake for 20–30 minutes, then leave to cool.

12. Garnish the braised emu with fresh saltbush (if available) or parsley and serve with freshly baked damper.

ALL YOU NEED IS LOVE & a good CUP OF COFFEE

'People love the nostalgia of it – we're the most photographed van wherever we go! I think it makes people happy to see it.'
Jade Morcom-Phoenix, owner

ORANGE & ALMOND CAKE

LITTLE BONNIE DOT, MULLUMBIMBY, AUSTRALIA

Jade Morcom-Phoenix was looking for a special project when a friend showed her photos of a vintage 1930s teardrop caravan. She bought it on the spot, and Little Bonnie Dot was born. The van had already been converted to house a commercial coffee machine, so all Jade had to do was give it a paint job and get baking to bring her vision for a mobile tea party to life. Making use of her collection of vintage china, Jade now serves high tea at markets, festivals and private events in Northern NSW and the Gold Coast. Classics such as jam drops, brownies and scones - 'the kind of recipes Nanna used to make' - are mainstays but it's this (gluten- and dairy-free) orange and almond cake that's become a favourite. The home-baked treats are served with coffee from Mullumbimby roaster The Branches, organic teas and turmeric lattes - and a dollop of retro charm.

Follow them on
Instagram: @little.bonnie.dot
Facebook: www.facebook.com/little.bonnie.dot

How to make it

🌿 SERVES 14/16

Ingredients
3 navel oranges
6 free-range eggs
1 tsp vanilla extract
200g (7oz) demerara sugar
225g (8oz) ground almonds
50g (1½oz) sunflower seeds
50g (1½oz) linseed or flax

To decorate:
1 navel orange
185g (6½oz) honey
   (or demerara sugar)
120ml (4fl oz) water
50g (2oz) flaked almonds

Method
1. Place the oranges in a pan and cover with water. Bring to the boil, reduce the heat and simmer for 1 hour. Drain, and repeat the process, then set aside to cool.

2. Preheat the oven to 180°C (350°F) and line a 30cm (12in) round or square cake tin with baking paper.

3. When the oranges are cool, place them in a food processor and blend to a puree.

4. Add the[...] add the va[...] LSA and ble[...]

5. Pour the b[...] bake for 1 hou[...] light golden or[...]

6. Meanwhile, slice the remaining orange and place it in a pan with the honey and water. Simmer until a syrup forms.

7. Pour the syrup over the warm cake, then decorate with the orange slices and sliced almonds.

SPICED SQUASH & KALE EMPANADAS

LITTLE WAHACA, GOLD COAST, AUSTRALIA

An eye for detail, exacting standards and culinary curiosity have made Little Wahaca a staple on the food-truck scene from Byron Bay to Brisbane. Chef Trent Mitchell launched his vintage-style caravan in 2016, fulfilling a long-held dream to dish up his take on Latin American food, first sparked on a trip through Mexico in his early twenties. Working from his tiny mobile kitchen, Trent makes as much as he can from scratch, including zingy sauces and marinades and hand-pressed *gorditas* (a puffy, crunchy taco), and any elements that are bought in, such as tortillas, come from local suppliers who prioritise high-quality, organic ingredients. However, that doesn't mean Trent is a total traditionalist - he enjoys being creative with the classics, and has found a niche in creating vegan versions of usually meat-heavy meals, like these spiced squash empanadas made with coconut oil.

Follow them on
Instagram: @littlewahaca
Facebook: www.facebook.com/LittleWahaca

© LITTLE WAHACA

How to make it

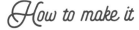

SERVES 4

Ingredients
vegetable oil, for frying

For the pastry:
115g (4oz) plain flour
30g (2 heaped tbs) coconut oil
pinch of salt
5 tsp cold water
1 tsp dry sherry vinegar
5 tsp dry sherry
5 tsp coconut milk

For the spiced squash & kale filling:
200g (7oz) butternut squash, diced
50ml (2fl oz) olive oil
30g (generous 1oz) cumin seeds, toasted & ground
salt & ground black pepper, to taste
½ brown onion, diced
1 garlic clove, finely chopped
4 large kale leaves, finely torn

For the tomatillo salsa:
100g (3¾oz) canned tomatillos, drained
1 garlic clove
1 fresh jalapeño pepper, seeded
1 tbs chopped coriander leaves & stems
50ml (2fl oz) olive oil
salt & ground black pepper, to taste

Method
1. To make the dough, mix the flour, oil and salt until crumbly. In a separate bowl, combine the water, vinegar and sherry. Add the liquid to the flour mix and knead until you have a smooth dough. Wrap in clear film and refrigerate for 1 hour.

2. Meanwhile, to make the filling, preheat the oven to 180°C (350°F). Toss the squash with most of the oil, cumin, salt and pepper on a roasting tray and roast for 20–30 minutes, until tender.

3. Saute the onion and garlic in the remaining oil for 10 minutes on low, then add the kale and cook until soft.

4. Combine the kale mixture with the squash, mash slightly, then set aside to cool.

5. To make the salsa, place all the ingredients in a blender and process until smooth.

6. Heat the oil in a deep-fryer or large frying pan.

7. Roll out the dough on a lightly floured surface until about 5mm (¼in) thick. Use a round, 12cm (4½in) pastry cutter to cut four rounds.

8. Place a spoonful of filling in the centre of each, fold over the pastry to create a semicircle, and seal the edges with your fingers or a fork, using coconut milk to bind.

9. Fry for 1–2 minutes per side on medium-high heat or until light golden. Drain and serve with salsa.

RAS EL HANOUT HALLOUMI KEBAB

MAMA TAHINA, AUCKLAND, NEW ZEALAND

Having grown up in England, Marc Hershman discovered a love for food during his travels after school, when he worked in a kibbutz in Israel baking bread and then explored various North African countries, where his interest in spices grew. Fast-forward a few years and Marc and his wife Cecilia had a desire to use good-quality ingredients to produce bold Mediterranean-type street food; so Mama Tahina was born. The food truck industry was small in New Zealand back in 2014, which meant the fit-out took longer than expected, but they finally launched in September 2015. Their menu includes rice bowls, gourmet kebabs, vegan schnitzels and seasonal salads, and their bright red truck appears at events around New Zealand. Ras el hanout, after which the dish is named, is a fragrant Moroccan spice mix that transports you to North Africa and, combined with pomegranate molasses and chermoula, elevates the kebab to a new level.

Follow them on
Instagram: @mamatahina
Facebook: www.facebook.com/mamatahina

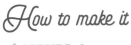

How to make it

🌿 SERVES 4

Ingredients

1 tbs ras el hanout
1 tsp sumac
5 tbs olive oil
250g (9oz) halloumi, cut into
    1½cm (³/₅in) slices
2 red onions, skin on, quartered
3 tbs pomegranate molasses
salt & ground black pepper, to
    taste

For the slaw:

¼ red cabbage, thinly sliced
¼ white cabbage, thinly sliced
1 red onion, thinly sliced
25g (1oz) parsley leaves, chopped
25g (1oz) mint leaves, chopped
25g (1oz) coriander leaves, chopped
juice of ½ lemon
2 tbs white wine vinegar
drizzle of olive oil
3 tbs pomegranate molasses
salt & ground black pepper, to
    taste

To serve:

2 tbs chermoula
5 tbs plain yoghurt
4 tbs buckwheat groats
4 warm laffa or flatbreads
4 tbs pomegranate molasses
pinch of microgreens
4 tbs pomegranate seeds
pickles of your choice

Method

1. Preheat the oven to 180°C (350°F).

2. Mix together the ras el hanout, sumac and 2 tbs of the oil, add the halloumi and turn to coat. Marinate for 1 hour and reserve.

3. Drizzle the remaining oil into a flameproof roasting pan and add the onions, skin side up. Season and roast for 35 minutes, turning halfway through.

4. Remove from the oven, carefully remove the skin and add the molasses. Place the pan on the hob and reduce the liquid to a glaze.

5. For the slaw, combine all the ingredients in a bowl.

6. For the toppings, combine the chermoula and yoghurt, and toast the buckwheat for 4–5 minutes in a dry, hot pan.

7. Heat a griddle or frying pan until very hot, then add the halloumi to bar mark both sides.

8. Add half the marinade, reduce the heat and cook until the halloumi is soft.

9. Place a small handful of slaw in a line in the middle of the bread, top with 3 pieces of halloumi and drizzle chermoula-yoghurt mix and molasses over the top. Add microgreens, pomegranate seeds and buckwheat. Serve with pomegranate onion and pickles of your choice on the side.

'*Hapunan* means "dinner", a reminder of the most important time of the day in the Filipino culture.'
Laura Tabora, co-owner

FILIPINO ADOBO DEL DIABLO

HAPUNAN, AUCKLAND, NEW ZEALAND

Aldrin Tabora, an industrial engineer, came to New Zealand from the Philippines seeking work but instead found something far more meaningful: a passion for food. He went on to study culinary arts and, together with his fiancée Laura, dreamed of one day owning a food truck. On a trip to the Philippines to meet Aldrin's family, Laura fell in love with the smiling Filipino people, their loving culture and delicious cuisine, and in 2017 the pair decided to use their wedding savings to buy and fit out a truck selling Filipino-inspired food. Easily recognisable, thanks to its tropical banana-leaf print, the truck mostly caters for meat lovers. Their best-selling dish is *adobo del diablo*, a chicken dish traditionally cooked with soy sauce and vinegar that has been modified by the duo to include coconut milk and chilli. It's commonly served with jasmine or garlic-fried rice, but at Hapunan they prefer coconut rice and slaw.

Follow them on
Instagram: @Hapunan
Facebook: www.facebook.com/HapunanFilipinoCuisine

How to make it

SERVES 4

Ingredients
100ml (3½fl oz) rice or
    coconut vinegar
425ml (15fl oz) coconut milk
4 tbs light soy sauce
5 garlic cloves, bruised
6 bird's-eye chillies
1 tsp ground turmeric
5 bay leaves
1kg (2¼lb) boneless, skinless
    chicken thighs
salt & ground black pepper,
    to taste
coconut rice & slaw, to serve

Method
1. In a large bowl combine the vinegar, coconut milk, soy sauce, garlic cloves, chillies, turmeric and bay leaves.

2. Add the chicken and massage the mixture into the meat. Cover with clear film and leave to marinate overnight in the fridge.

3. Transfer the chicken to a large, deep pan and bring to the boil.

4. Simmer for 25 minutes or until the chicken is cooked through.

5. Lift out the c[...] slotted spoon [...] clean dish to re[...] sauce in the po[...]

6. Simmer the sauce to reduce it until a thick gravy is achieved.

7. Discard the bay leaves and chillies, and season to taste.

8. Serve with coconut rice and slaw.

PERUVIAN SACHA TACO

HIT 'N RUN, LIMA, PERU

One of the first food trucks in Peru, Hit 'n Run has creativity as its driving force. Unique ingredients representative of the diverse regions of Peru pop up on the menu, which seems to change as often as the chalk graphics decorating the truck. The owner, Mariano Escobal, puts into play ingredients that are rarely consumed in the capital city, making the culinary experience as surprising for locals as it is for foreign visitors. One week the menu will list three variations of the classic late-night snack *salchipapas* (fried wedges of Peruvian potatoes topped with hot dog slices), and the next, wraps inspired by exotic flavours of the Amazon or a Northern Peru edition, full of tender beef, corn and fried plantain. During the summer months (January–March), Hit 'n Run can be found in Lima's popular beach district, Asia. The rest of the year they do pop-ups at events.

Follow them on
Instagram: @hitnrunfoodtruck
Facebook: www.facebook.com/hitnrunfoodtruck

How to make it

SERVES 4

Ingredients
4 tbs oil
1 tbs chopped garlic
2 tbs finely chopped white onion
150g (5oz) *cecina* (dried meat), chopped
3 tbs tomato paste
2 tomatoes, skinned, seeded & chopped
500ml (17fl oz) beef broth
2 bay leaves
salt & ground black pepper, to taste
2 *coconas* (tropical citrus fruit), peeled & cubed
115g (4oz) pineapple, peeled & cubed
juice of 3 lemons
1 tbs chopped *sacha culantro* (leaves of long coriander)
3 tbs mayonnaise
5 tbs coconut milk
4 corn tortillas

Method
1. Put the oil in a pan and place over low heat. Add the garlic, onion and *cecina* and cook for about 5 minutes, stirring occasionally.

2. Add the tomato paste, tomatoes, broth and bay leaves and cook for 30 minutes.

3. Season to taste with salt and pepper, then remove from the heat and set aside.

4. In a separate bowl, mix the *cocona*, pineapple, lemon juice and *sacha culantro*. Season to taste and set aside.

5. In another bowl, blend the mayonnaise and coconut milk, then season to taste and chill for 20 minutes.

6. Heat the corn tortillas on a griddle for 30 seconds.

7. Plate a tortilla and add some of the *cecina* mixture, top with *cocona* and pineapple slaw and the coconut mayonnaise. Roll or fold the taco and serve.

'The idea is that each dish we serve is a collision of creativity and spontaneity ... a fusion of flavours from Peru and around the world.'
Mariano Escobal, owner

'Our aim is to transmit a strong Peruvian feeling. As the name Lima Sabrosa ("flavourful Lima") suggests, Lima is a city where many different cultures and flavours merge.'
Natalia Miori, co-owner

THE CAJACHA

burger with mushrooms & cheese

LIMA SABROSA, LIMA, PERU

Since 2013, Natalia Miori and Alejandro Acuña have been flipping homestyle patties topped with native ingredients that represent Peru's diverse cultural mix. Their juicy, bold-flavoured burgers have become popular in Lima, where their flashy truck highlighting iconic chicha graphic art rambles between Jirón Portocarrero in Surquillo and other pop-up locations. Their most popular item is the Cajacha burger, featuring distinctive porcon mushrooms and salty Andino cheese, which originate in the Andes. While it'd be difficult to replicate the exact flavours elsewhere, they can be substituted by other dried mushrooms (porcini, portobello, shiitake) and any white cheese that will melt when exposed to heat. And some last words of advice from a burger expert: 'To avoid a soggy burger, the pan needs to be super hot. This way the patty develops a thick crust on the outside that will keep the juices from escaping. *¡Ese es el tip!* (That's the secret!)'

Follow them on
Instagram: @limasabrosahamburguesas
Facebook: www.facebook.com/limasabrosa

How to make it

SERVES 1

Ingredients
40g (1½oz) dried mushrooms
salt, to taste
150g (5oz) minced beef
ground black pepper, to taste
hamburger bun
2 slices of Swiss cheese
handful of shredded lettuce
1 tomato, sliced

Method
1. Soak the dried mushrooms for 30 minutes.

2. Drain, then add half to a blender and blend until smooth. Pour the mixture into a bowl and combine with the remaining mushrooms. Add a pinch of salt.

3. Heat a frying pan or skillet on high heat.

4. Put the beef in a bowl, add salt and pepper, combine and form into a patty about 1cm thick so it cooks evenly.

5. Place the burger on the heated pan and cook for 2 minutes per side.

6. When the burger is nearly done, place the bun halves on the pan to crisp and warm.

7. Place the patty on one half of the bun and top with mushrooms and cheese. Add the lettuce and tomato and place the other bun half on top.

'All of our recipes are created by our chef, Mune, so you won't be able to taste something like it anywhere else!'
Augusto Velez, co-owner

YAKISOBA BOWL

LUCA CHINA, LIMA, PERU

Peruvian slang for 1 sol and 50 centimos - a common price for boarding a city bus - *luca china* is food-truck speak for really good yakisoba. Based in Lima, a city with a vast Chinese and Japanese population, Luca China serves to crowds whose cravings venture to the East. Think sautéed vegetables (*yasaitame*), deep-fried gyozas, and thick buckwheat noodles (*yakisoba*). Having opened in 2016, Luca China's menu is what separates the young competitor from the rest in the local scene. 'Since one of our founders [Mune] is a chef, we knew we wanted to start a business in the world of gastronomy,' says Augusto Velez, who co-founded the truck with two friends. 'We were intrigued by the growing popularity of food trucks and noticed that there weren't any trucks in Lima offering nikkei [Japanese-Peruvian fusion]. That, and the fact that Mune has Japanese ancestry, became our inspiration for the menu.'

Follow them on
Instagram: @lucachinaft
Facebook: www.facebook.com/lucachinaft

How to make it

SERVES 1 (LARGE) OR 2 (SMALL)

Ingredients
200g (7oz) soba noodles
2 tbs oyster sauce
1 tsp soy sauce
1 tsp sugar
3 tsp vegetable oil
150g (5oz) chicken, beef, pork or a mixture (depending on preference)
½ onion, roughly chopped
½ red bell pepper, roughly chopped
25g (1oz) bok choy (or cabbage), roughly chopped
15g (½oz) mangetouts
1 tsp grated fresh root ginger
salt, to taste
1 tsp sesame oil
sriracha chilli sauce or other hot sauce (optional)

Method
1. Cook the soba noodles according to packet instructions, then strain and toss in cold water. Drain and set aside.

2. In a small bowl, whisk together the oyster sauce, soy sauce and sugar, th

3. Heat a frying pan or wok on medium-high and add the oil.

4. Add your preferred protein to the pan and sauté until fully cooked.

5. Add the onion, bell pepper, bok choy and mangetouts along with the meat and toss for a few seconds, allowing the veggies to heat up.

6. Add the noodles, ginger and oyster sauce mixture, continuing to toss and sauté together for a minute or two. Adjust the seasoning if necessary.

7. Finally, add the sesame oil and chilli sauce, if using, and sauté for 1 more minute, then serve.

'Food trucks are able to stay innovative, bringing exceptional food, whether it's casual or gourmet, to a greater public with a smaller investment.'
Sandra Millan, chef & founder

MARTÍN ARGENTINO
(Argentine sandwich)

EL VAGABUNDO, BOGOTÁ, COLOMBIA

Having spent five years in New York studying at The Culinary Institute of America and putting her lessons into practice at the likes of Eataly and Rouge Tomate, Sandra Millan found inspiration on the streets of the Big Apple. 'It was a time when the food trucks were booming', notes the chef. After graduating, the native Colombian returned to Bogotá, where she opened her own food truck, El Vagabundo. Using local ingredients, the menu features flavours from around the world. Easy to eat on the go, the variety of sandwiches brings new gastronomic experiences in a familiar package. From 'Martin,' a ciabatta stuffed with Argentine influences, to 'Kim,' a pork bahn-mi full of sweet and tangy layers so typical of the Vietnamese classic, El Vagabundo takes eaters on a sensory tour around the globe. Regularly parked inside the US Embassy in Bogotá, El Vagabundo can also be found at various events citywide.

Follow them on
Instagram: @elvagabundocol
Facebook: www.facebook.com/elvagabundotruck

How to make it

SERVES 1

Ingredients
1 tbs vegetable oil
1 tbs butter
½ white or yellow onion, peeled & thinly sliced
pinch of salt
1 ciabatta roll
½ roasted pepper, drained and sliced
150g (5oz) flank steak
2 tbs chimichurri
2 slices of Gouda
plantain or yuca chips, to serve
suero costeño (or sour cream), to serve

Method
1. Heat the oil and butter in a frying pan over a low-medium heat, add the onions and salt and cook slowly for 20–25 minutes, stirring occasionally, until golden and caramelised.

2. Meanwhile, warm the ciabatta roll in the oven, then slice in half.

3. Add the pepper to the onions and heat through.

4. Heat a grill pan or skillet on high until on the verge of smoking. Reduce the heat to medium-high and place the steak on the pan. Cook for 3 minutes on each side for a medium finish, then remove from the pan and leave to rest for 5–7 minutes.

5. Thinly slice the steak, then place on one half of ciabatta. Top with the onions, pepper, chimichurri and gouda. Place the remaining ciabatta half on top.

6. Serve with plantain or yuca chips and *suero costeño*, a traditional sauce likened to sour cream that originates from the Colombian coast.

URUGUAYAN FLAN

MERCE DAGLIO, MONTEVIDEO, URUGUAY

When Mercedes Daglio was a child she would race her siblings for the best pancakes and compete to see who flipped them best. Soaking up her mother's confectionery skills, she deepened her expertise in one of Uruguay's most prestigious culinary schools. Then, while on holiday, Mercedes and her partner visited a food truck fair and decided to launch their own. And so the quest for the perfect truck began. When they got wind of an old 1978 gas delivery truck that was roaming the streets of a nearby region, they set off to rescue the clunker and, eight months later, the Sweet Truck was born. Like most food truckers in Uruguay, Mercedes sells at food fairs and various events on the capital's cultural agenda. Customers can't seem to get enough of her *alfajorcitos de maicena*, a sandwich cookie filled with dulce de leche and covered in coconut flakes, and this flan.

Follow them on Instagram: @mercedagliorepostería

How to make it

SERVES 8/10

Ingredients

1L (1¾ pints) milk
400g (14oz) sugar, plus 4 tbs for the caramel
6 eggs
1 tsp vanilla extract
1 tsp salt

Method

1. Put the milk and 400g (14oz) of the sugar in a pan, bring to the boil and let it boil until it turns a caramel colour. Set aside to cool. Preheat the oven to 160°C (325°F).

2. Make a caramel by melting the 4 tbs of sugar in a small stainless-steel pan (don't use a non-stick pan or it won't work) over low-medium heat, swirling it occasionally until the sugar melts. Do not stir or it will crystalise. Carry on cooking the syrup until it turns a caramel colour, then immediately remove from the heat. Handle it carefully as it will be very hot. Pour the caramel into a flan dish (or flanera), covering the sides evenly.

3. One by one, add the eggs to the cooled milk mixture, then stir in the vanilla and salt.

4. Strain the mixture and pour it over the caramel in the flan dish.

5. Cover the flan dish with tinfoil, place it in a larger baking tray and pour boiling water into the tray to come halfway up the sides of the flan dish.

6. Bake for 35 minutes, then take off the tinfoil and bake for 15 minutes more.

7. Check that the centre is set, remove the flan from the oven and refrigerate overnight.

TAPÍ PARRÍ (TAPIOCA PANCAKE)

filled with brie, toasted almonds & truffle honey

TAPÍ TAPIOCA, RIO DE JANEIRO, BRAZIL

The Brazilian food truck scene exploded in 2014 after legislation was passed to allow them to operate in the largest cities. But while most Rio-based trucks sell conventional fast-food with US or European roots, Marianna Ferolla decided hers, Tapí Tapioca, would sell something 100% Brazilian. Tapioca is the starch extracted from the cassava root, a vegetable native to Brazil, which has long been used as a staple food. Tapioca is also the name given to the stuffed pancakes Marianna believes will one day conquer the world. The chewy texture of the tapioca works brilliantly with melted cheese and this accounts for the popularity of the Tapí Parrí, a combination of creamy Brie, crunchy almonds and fragrant truffle honey. In 2016, the Tapí team opened their first store and since then have opened several other venues. 'Eventually we'd like to expand Tapí internationally', smiles Marianna, 'But one step at a time.'

Follow them on
Instagram: @tapitapioca

How to make it

🌿 SERVES 2

Ingredients
120g (5oz) tapioca starch powder (not pearls or granules)
water, to hydrate
2g (pinch) salt
150g (6oz) Brie, cut into 2cm (1in) cubes
40g (1½oz) toasted flaked almonds
2 tbs truffle honey

Method

1. Place the tapioca starch in a small bowl and gradually add water, mixing as you go. Keep adding more water until the starch is totally saturated, forming a uniform mass. Cover and leave the starch to settle for 2 hours.

2. Dab off any excess surface moisture with kitchen paper, then scoop the starch into a sieve placed over a large bowl. Rub the lumps through with a spoon. The starch will be transformed into a fine, damp powder. Mix in the salt.

3. Heat a small frying pan over a medium–high heat for 2 minutes. For the first pancake, sprinkle in a 5mm (¼in) layer of the starch powder, covering the entire surface (use the back of a spoon to spread the powder evenly).

4. After 2 minutes, the powder will have gelled together to form a single pancake. Flip to cook the other side for 30 seconds, then flip back again.

5. Place half the quantity of the Brie cubes in an even layer covering one half of the pancake. Sprinkle over half the almonds, drizzle with the half honey and fold the pancake in two.

6. Cook for another 30 seconds so the cheese starts to melt, then slide on to a plate and serve. Repeat for your second pancake.

121

'When I travel, I like to eat local food. When I'm in Italy, I'm not looking for Mexican food. I want to eat foods that make Italy special and I want to eat what the locals are eating.'
Ashley McNamee, owner

BLACK COD TIPS & JASMINE RICE

ASHMO'S, SITKA, USA

Ashley McNamee, proprietor of Ashmo's, was reticent about naming her truck after herself, but once she visualised the creative label – her high-school nickname in the shape of a fish – she went for it. The truck, usually located by the Coliseum Theatre in Sitka, is one of only a couple on Baranof Island. McNamee found the truck, a former uniform delivery vehicle, deconstructed in Portland, and fitted it out with new equipment. An experienced chef with a culinary degree from New York, McNamee says she found the concept easy: showcasing locally caught fish. The menu includes rockfish tacos, beer-battered fish and chips, a lingcod sandwich and smoked salmon mac 'n' cheese, which was rated among Alaska's top 10 mac and cheeses in 2018. But the most unique item? Black cod tips served over coconut coriander rice. The tips are located in the collars of sablefish, and prepared to Ashmo's special recipe.

Follow them on
Facebook: www.facebook.com/Ashmos-838731282868741/

How to make it

SERVES 2

Ingredients

225g (½lb) black cod tips (or fillets of sablefish/butterfish cut into chunks, or substitute with an oily fish, such as salmon belly or Chilean sea bass)
½ tsp vegetable oil

For the teriyaki marinade:
500ml (17½fl oz) soy sauce
225ml (8fl oz) water
½ tbs garlic puree
25g (1oz) soft light brown sugar
½ tbs cornflour

For the rice:
100g (3½ oz) rice
170ml (6fl oz) water
60ml (2fl oz) unsweetened coconut milk
½ tbs butter
½ tbs olive oil
1½ tbs coconut flakes
1 tbs sugar
1½ tbs chopped coriander leaves

Method

1. For the marinade, put the soy sauce, water, garlic and sugar in a pa... and bri...

2. Mix th... with a litt... whisk it in... for at leas... ...g, until smooth and thick.

3. Put the fish in a dish and pour over the marinade. Cover, place in the fridge and leave to marinate overnight.

4. To cook the fish, put the oil in a frying pan and place over medium heat. Add the fish, shaking off excess marinade, and cook for 4–5 minutes, moving the fish around to cook off excess liquid so the fish can get nicely browned.

5. For the rice, put everything apart from the coriander in a rice cooker and prepare as normal, or place in a pan and cook for about 10 minutes, until done. Stir in the chopped coriander just before serving, and lay the fish pieces on top.

'Salmon is what Alaska is known for. To me it's awesome: it's healthy – full of omega 3 fatty acids – and it's delicious.'
Dave McCasland, owner

SALMON 'N' CHIPS

DECKHAND DAVE'S, JUNEAU, USA

Given the truck's name, it's no surprise to learn that owner Dave McCasland earned his culinary stripes while working as a deckhand and chief cook on a fishing vessel in Alaskan waters. Armed with a love for sustainable fishing methods, a degree in chemistry and thousands of hours at sea, in May 2016 he opened his truck, a converted trailer (these days it's a permanent fixture between May and September on the downtown Juneau waterfront). Dave and his staff whip up scrumptious seafood dishes: salmon 'n' chips, tacos stuffed with beer-battered halibut, blackened rockfish, and breaded salmon - an ultra-popular choice. Fried salmon is best served with perfectly fried chips (fries), a wedge of lemon and zingy tartar sauce. Dave's sauce recipe is secret, but he's happy to reveal the ideal salmon method: cooking it until it's slightly crispy on the outside and exactly 52°C (125°F) in the centre.

**Follow them on
Instagram:** @Deckhanddavesfishtacos

How to make it

SERVES 4

Ingredients
4 medium potatoes
2 salmon fillets, about 2¼kg (5lb)
50g (2oz) salt
50g (2oz) soft light brown sugar
50g (2oz) plain flour
8 eggs, beaten
450g (1lb) panko breadcrumbs
2¼L (4 pints) avocado oil
1 lemon, quartered, to serve
tartare sauce, to serve

Method
1. First, start the chips. Cut the potatoes into 1cm (½in) strips and blanch them in a pan of boiling water for 2 minutes. Rinse under cold water, lay on a baking sheet and freeze for 30 minutes.

2. Remove the skin from the salmon and slice the fillets into large strips.

3. To brine the salmon strips, rub in salt on the outside of each strip, then toss them in brown sugar. Allow to sit on a plate for about 15 minutes until the brine has dissolved. Shake off the excess.

4. Dus... flour, ... off th... strip...

5. Heat ... heavy pan (note: other oils c... be used but their 'smoke point' is different), to 200°C (400°F). Cook the chips until golden, then drain on kitchen paper.

6. Fry the fish in the oil for 1½–2 minutes, turning once, until golden brown. Drain on kitchen paper and serve with the chips, a lemon wedge and a generous dollop of tartare sauce.

TUNA TACOS

TACOFINO, TOFINO, CANADA

Food trucks don't come much more remote than Tacofino. Located on the wild west coast of Tofino on Vancouver Island in Canada, Tacofino has been serving up the tastiest tacos to surfers since it opened its van doors in 2009. Inspired by bold flavours and back-alley BBQs from around the world, it wanted to serve up something simple to the surfers rolling in off the beach - tacos like you've never had before. Starting from humble beginnings in the Live to Surf parking lot, they now have six restaurants and three food trucks around Vancouver and Vancouver Island, though nothing can beat the original for its location. Their fresh tuna tacos with pico de gallo and wasabi mayo are delicious, and it's the use of simple ingredients treated well that has made Tacofino such a success.

Follow them on Instagram: @tacofinovan

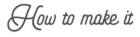

How to make it

SERVES 4

Ingredients
4 x 15cm (6in) flour tortillas
225g (8oz) albacore tuna loin
pinch of salt
20g (¾oz) pickled ginger
20g (¾oz) wakame

For the pico de gallo:
1 bull heart tomato, chopped
2 tbs chopped white onion
1 tsp brown sugar
1 tsp salt
1 tbs chopped coriander leaves
1 tsp chopped pickled jalapeño
    peppers
1 tsp pickled jalapeño juice
juice of 1 lime

For the soy glaze:
1 tbs sugar
1 garlic clove
½ Thai chilli
50ml (2fl oz) soy sauce
4 tsp water
4 drops of sesame oil
1 tsp potato starch or cornflour
1 tbs chopped coriander leaves
juice of ½ lime

For the wasabi mayo:
1 tbs mayo

squeeze of lime juice
wasabi paste, to taste

Method
1. To make the pico de gallo, put the tomato and onion in a bowl. Season with sugar and salt, then add the rest of the ingredients, mix and set aside.

2. To prepare the soy glaze, put the sugar, garlic and chilli in a small pan. Melt the sugar over low heat and wait until it turns golden brown. Add the soy sauce, water and sesame oil, bring to a boil, then add the potato starch or cornflour and stir until it thickens. Add the coriander and lime juice, let it sit for 3 minutes, then strain it into a bowl.

3. To make the wasabi mayo, whisk all the ingredients together.

4. Grill the tortillas on both sides. Set aside.

5. Slice the tuna into four pieces. Season, then grill or sear on high heat, cooking to your preference.

6. Place one piece of tuna on each tortilla, glaze with the soy glaze, and top with the wasabi mayo and pico de gallo. Sprinkle with pickled ginger and wakame, roll up and enjoy.

'I'm not a chef, I don't even cook at home. But my ideas (for new products) keep coming and coming.'
Noriki Tamura, co-owner

OROSHI HOT DOG

JAPADOG, VANCOUVER, CANADA

Until recently, Vancouver laws prohibited the sale of street food - except hot dogs. Husband-and-wife entrepreneurs Noriki and Misa Tamura turned that restriction into a novel product and in 2005, after emigrating from Japan, they launched Japadog, a food truck offering hot dogs with Japanese flavours. Even in the now-thriving food truck scene, Japadog continues to draw line-ups, particularly for its signature terimayo, a hot dog topped with teriyaki sauce, mayonnaise and seaweed, and *oroshi*, mounded with daikon. There's also the negimiso turkey dog with shredded cabbage and miso sauce, okonomi pork sausage with *okonomiyaki* (Japanese pancakes), and a yakisoba hot dog with stir-fried noodles. Noriki says you'd never see this style of hot dog in Japan - they're his invention - but in a city where nearly half the population is of Asian heritage, this Japanese-Canadian hybrid is fulfilling Japadog's mission: 'delivering dreams, happiness, and excitement to the world - through hot dogs.'

Follow them on
Instagram: @japadog.canada
Twitter: @japadog

How to make it

SERVES 4

Ingredients
4 bratwurst or other sausage
4 hot dog buns
250ml (8fl oz) *oroshi* (grated daikon or mooli)
green onions, thinly sliced, to taste
usukuchi (light soy sauce), to taste

Method
1. To prepare the bratwurst, put them in a frying pan or griddle pan and cook over medium-high heat for around 15 minutes.

2. Place the sausages in the buns. Place a thin layer of *oroshi* over each sausage, covering the entire surface.

3. Sprinkle with green onions, then sprinkle with *usukuchi*, so it covers most of the *oroshi*.

'My spirit animal is an Italian grandmother. Regular customers call me "nonna". I want to host, entertain, and be sure that everyone leaves well fed. *Mangia! Mangia!*'
Rachael May Grossman,
founder & chef

POLPO ALLA GRIGLIA

(grilled octopus)

ARTIGIANO, PORTLAND, USA

In Portland, Oregon, Artigiano has charted its own distinct culinary direction. Unlike most of the trucks, which hang around like whales in groups called pods, Artigiano floats solo in a quiet part of East Portland. And whereas meals offered at most trucks are of the grab-and-go variety, Artigiano offers a traditional sit-down experience, with an ever-changing menu based on seasonal availability from local farmers and the whims of its creator and chef, Rachael May Grossman. Inspired by the way food is served and shared in Italy, Rachael's concept was to bring to Portland an authentic Italian osteria - complete with outdoor, courtyard, multicourse dinners, fine Italian wines and occasional live jazz. Artigiano is open from May to mid-October, allowing Rachael to travel back to Italy to gain fresh inspiration. Though Artigiano keeps a small à la carte menu, most diners simply allow Rachael to cook complete meals for them.

**Follow them on
Facebook:** www.facebook.com/artigianopdx

How to make it

SERVES 16

Ingredients
1 whole 2.25–3.2kg (5–7lb) octopus, beak removed
5 bay leaves
475ml (16fl oz) white or rosé wine
3 garlic cloves, smashed
1 tbs whole black peppercorns
1 lemon, cut in half
50ml (2fl oz) olive oil
lemon wedges, to serve

Method
1. Put all the ingredients in a very large pan.

2. Cover with extra water, as needed, so the octopus is fully submerged.

3. Cover and bring to a simmer over medium heat, or cover and bake in an oven preheated to 180°C (350°F), for 2 hours or until the octopus will cut easily with a butter knife.

4. Strain off the liquid (reserve it to use as stock for another dish) and chill the octopus.

5. Preheat griddle pan to high. Cut the octopus tentacles and add them to the pan. Sear it all over.

6. Serve with lemon wedges. *Buon appetite!*

'I wish I had a better story, but I got wasted at 4am and that's how I came up with the name of the truck. It's cheeky fun – food trucks allow you to do that.'
Han Ly Hwang, owner

KOREAN JAPCHAE BANCHAN

KIM JONG GRILLIN', PORTLAND, USA

In Portland, Oregon, the global economic crisis helped pave the way for a boomlet of extra-small restaurants - food trucks - which cropped up in parking lots all over the city. Competition was fierce, but Han Ly Hwang's Korean cart, Kim Jong Grillin', won a faithful following early on. His success, however, was short-lived as his business was incinerated in an accidental fire just 10 months after opening. Happily for bibim fans, though, Hwang persevered and reopened a few years later. While the name is tongue-in-cheek, Kim Jong Grillin' takes its Korean food seriously - dishes are inspired by the home cooking Hwang ate growing up. The signature item on the menu is the so-called 'bibim box', a takeaway spin on the bibimbap - a rice base with veggies, meat, kimchi and a soft egg on top. KJG has two locations in town: 4606 SE Division St and 1207 SE Hawthorne Blvd.

**Follow them on
Facebook:** www.facebook.com/kjgpdx

How to make it

🌿 **SERVES 4**

Ingredients
450g (1lb) dang myun noodles
1 tsp vegetable oil
3 carrots, julienned
1 large sweet onion, julienned
1 red bell pepper, julienned
2 bunches of spring onions, cut into long strips
450g (1lb) fresh shiitake mushrooms (or oyster mushrooms), cut into strips
120ml (4fl oz) sesame oil
120ml (4fl oz) soy sauce
225g (8oz) spinach leaves

Method
1. Boil the noodles according to the packet instructions, then strain and set aside in a large bowl.

2. Heat the oil in a large frying pan over medium heat, then add the carrot, sweet onion, pepper and spring onion and sauté for about 5 minutes or until al dente – do not overcook. Add to the noodles in the bowl and set aside.

3. Cook the mushrooms in the frying pan with a little of the sesame oil and about 3 tbs of soy sauce for 3–4 minutes, until tender. Add them to the noodles and vegetables.

4. Pour in the remaining sesame oil and the soy sauce and mix by hand to combine.

5. Cool the dish quickly in the freezer or fridge before serving – slow chilling will result in an unwanted sour taste.

THAI KHAO MAN GAI

NONG'S KHAO MAN GAI, PORTLAND, USA

No one personifies the American Dream better than Nong Poonsukwattana, who left her native Thailand with $70 and a couple of suitcases in 2003. Today, she's the owner of one of Portland's most successful food trucks (and a couple of brick-and-mortar locations), and is a mini culinary celebrity. As a contestant on the American TV competition *Chopped*, Nong earned notoriety by combining unlikely flavours and beating her opponents over three rounds. She's a woman of few words, but her fierce determination shines through. Her first kitchen was so tiny that she only had room to produce one dish: Khao Man Gai - succulent poached chicken served over rice that's found throughout Bangkok, with roots linked to Hainan Island. Her recipe has been such a success that it's still the only item she serves.

Follow them on Twitter @nongskhaomangai

How to make it

SERVES 4–5

Ingredients
1 large chicken
4½L (1 gallon) water
50g (2oz) sea salt
2 tbs sugar
1 garlic bulb
150g (6oz) fresh root ginger, thinly sliced
6 pandan leaves

For the rice:
3 tbs finely chopped garlic
8 tbs diced shallots, diced
200g (8oz) fresh root ginger, thinly sliced
25g (1oz) galangal, thinly sliced
3 pandan leaves
400g (14oz) jasmine rice

For the soup:
about 250g (9oz) Chinese winter squash flesh, cubed
4 tbs soy sauce
½ tsp ground white pepper
1 tbs chopped coriander leaves
1 tbs chopped green onion

To garnish:
cucumber strips
coriander leaves

Method

1. Remove the skin from the chicken and cook it in a pan until the fat renders out. Reserve.

2. Put the water, salt, sugar, garlic, ginger and pandan leaves in a pan and bring to the boil. Add the chicken and simmer for 35 minutes, until cooked. Lift out the chicken and keep warm. Reserve the stock.

3. For the rice, put 2 tbs of the rendered fat in a frying pan and add the garlic, shallots, ginger, galangal and pandan leaves. Fry until golden.

4. Stir in the rice and toast for 2 minutes. Add 1L (2 pints) of the stock, stir until it comes to the boil, then cover and simmer for 10–15 minutes.

5. For the soup, add the squash to the remaining stock, bring to the boil and cook for 15 minutes. Add the soy sauce, pepper, coriander leaves and onion.

6. To serve, cut the chicken into pieces. Divide the rice between bowls, ladle over soup and garnish with cucumbers and coriander.

137

'Our food was born of a desire to do something different yet authentic. That's what put us on the map: Indian food made with the intention of not scaring anybody.'
Akash Kapoor, founder and CEO

INDIAN STREET FOOD

CURRY UP NOW

CHANA MASALA

CURRY UP NOW, SAN FRANCISCO, USA

In 2009, just as the branded food truck revolution was gaining momentum, Akash Kapoor and his partners launched Curry Up Now in San Francisco. The mission was to serve authentic Indian food with traditional North Indian flavours, but in accessible ways that were also a touch atypical. Such was the genesis of their breakthrough Tikka Masala Burrito - a truck-friendly, eat-while-you-walk approach to Indian food that's familiar but cool and has a little bit of mystery. Since then, their Deconstructed Samosas, Naughty Naan, Sexy Fries and other signature specials have complemented a menu of classics, including Chana Masala, a chickpea curry mainstay. Just don't call anything fusion or modern food, because at heart it's true to time-honoured tastes, with ingredients that are, as much as possible, organic, locally sourced and environmentally conscious. Today, Curry Up Now reaches fans through its food truck, six Bay Area fine-casual restaurants and two Mortar & Pestle bars serving unique India-inspired cocktails.

Follow them on
Instagram: @curryupnow
Facebook: @CurryUpNow

ℋow to make it

🌿 **SERVES 4**

Ingredients
2 x 400g (14oz) cans chickpeas
1L (1¾ pints) water
2 teabags (preferably Red Label)
50ml (2fl oz) rapeseed oil or ghee
2 medium onions, finely chopped
1 tbs ginger garlic puree
pinch of salt
150g (5oz) tomato puree
juice of 1 lemon
2 tsp coriander leaves, chopped
cooked rice, to serve

For the spice blend:
2 tsp ground cumin
2 tsp ground coriander
½ tsp ground turmeric
1 tsp pomegranate seeds
2 cloves
2 black cardamoms
4 green cardamoms
½ stick cinnamon
2 small bay leaves
4 dried red chillies
salt, to taste

Method
1. Drain the chickpeas and put in a pan with the water and teabags. Bring to the boil, then turn off the heat and set aside for 10 minutes. Remove the teabags.

2. To make the spice blend, put all the ingredients in a dry frying pan and toast, shaking often, for 1–2 minutes, until fragrant. Transfer to a mortar and pestle or spice grinder and grind into fine powder.

3. Heat the oil or ghee in a frying pan, add the onion, ginger, garlic puree and salt and sauté for 8–10 minutes or until softened.

4. Stir in the spice blend and cook for 10 more minutes. Add 1 tbs of the chickpea water to prevent sticking.

5. Add the tomato puree and cook for 5 minutes.

6. Pour in the chickpeas and water. Cook for 20 minutes or until thickened, then stir in the lemon juice.

7. Garnish with fresh coriander and serve with rice.

'The kimchi quesadilla started as a fun food for us to enjoy in the truck and it just hit the streets with a force. Its spirit comes from Koreatown.'
Roy Choi, owner and chef

KIMCHI QUESADILLAS
with salsa verde

KOGI, LOS ANGELES, USA

It's no exaggeration to say that the transformation of American food trucks from 'roach coaches' to gourmet havens goes back to 2008, when Chef Roy Choi put Korean short ribs in tacos on the menu. A fusion revolution was born – and an only-in-LA one, given the city's giant Korean and Mexican communities. While the Kogi truck is still a mainstay of the LA street fair and late-night bar scene, the truck has travelled to music festivals all over and spawned a catering business, bar and the bricks-and-mortar restaurant, Chego. Roy is also scheduled to open a new restaurant in Las Vegas, where America's chef royalty is crowned.

Follow them on
Instagram @kogibbq
Twitter @kogibbq

How to make it

SERVES 4

Ingredients
225g (8oz) kimchi, chopped
115g (4oz) butter
4 tbs rapeseed oil
4 x 30cm (12in) flour tortillas
450g (1lb) Cheddar cheese, grated
8 sesame or shiso leaves
4 tbs roasted sesame seeds

For the salsa verde:
2L (3½ pints) rapeseed oil
1.2kg (2½lb) garlic cloves
1 yellow onion, peeled and quartered
10 jalapeño peppers, stemmed & halved
24 sprigs of coriander, cleaned & chopped coarsely
200g (7oz) toasted sesame seeds
200g (7oz) kosher salt
600ml (1 pint) fresh lime juice
600ml (1 pint) fresh orange juice

Method
1. For the salsa verde, put the oil in a large, deep pan over a medium heat. Add the garlic and confit slowly, stirring constantly, until deeply brown. Remove from the heat and leave to cool.

2. Char the onions and jalapeños until almost black under a preheated grill or over a flame. Leave to cool.

3. Put the oil, garlic, onion, jalapeños and all the other salsa verde ingredients in a food processor or blender and puree until smooth. Set aside.

4. Put the kimchi and butter in a frying pan and stir over medium heat for about 10 minutes, or until caramelised and charred.

5. Oil a pan or griddle, place a tortilla on it and sprinkle 115g (4oz) cheese on one half. Top the cheese with 50g (2oz) kimchi, two ripped sesame or shiso leaves and 1 tbs sesame seeds.

6. Fold over the tortilla to create a half moon shape.

7. Cook until the bottom is golden, then flip over and cook the other side. The quesadilla should look blistered. Remove to a plate and repeat the process.

8. Serve with the salsa verde.

141

BEER CHEESE & JALAPEÑO SPREAD

YEASTIE BOYS, LOS ANGELES, USA

'You've gotta fight … For your right … To … traditional Jewish round breads with fillings your bubbe never heard of!' could be the theme song for this truck with a punk vibe that's a perfect fit for LA; the menu lists bagels, lox, schmear and 'other sh*t'. Founded in 2014 by 'Bagel Lord' Evan Fox, Yeastie Boys stuffs its bagels with out-there yet tasty fillings - the Game Over sandwich starts with this beer-cheese and jalapeño spread and adds soft scrambled eggs, bacon and sliced tomato on a Cheddar bagel. A little more calming (but no less creative), the MILF puts plain cream cheese, sliced banana and Nutella on a plain bagel. Edgy though Yeastie Boys may be, their quality is old-world: hand-rolled bagels - in plain, poppy, sesame and more - baked each morning. You can find the truck parked outside some of LA's finest coffee shops.

Follow them on
Instagram: @yeastieboysbagels
Facebook: www.facebook.com/yeastieboysbagels

How to make it

SERVES 4

Ingredients
350ml (12fl oz) Pilsner beer
250g (9oz) small pickled jalapeño peppers, diced
1.3kg (3lb) cream cheese
350g (12oz) mild Cheddar cheese, finely grated
3 garlic cloves, finely chopped
4 tbs chilli powder

Method
1. Put the beer and jalapeños in a pan, bring to the boil, then simmer over medium heat until the liquid evaporates, stirring occasionally. Set aside to cool.

2. Put the chillies and all the other ingredients in a food processor and mix on low speed until the ingredients blend together.

3. Transfer to container and allow to sit in fridge overnight before use so the flavours can develop.

'For me it's really important to give you something that tastes great, that I woke up to cook for you from scratch that's fresh, amazing and nutritious.'
Sarina El, owner & chef

NEWPORT BOWL WITH TOFU

CALIFARMICATION, ORANGE COUNTY, USA

In 2017, after four soul-stifling years as a commercial real estate broker, Sarina El travelled with her mother to Cambodia, her parents' birth country. The goal was to discover (and perhaps tell) her mother's story by reconnecting with the culture, values and special affinity for large, complex meals. Inspired, El continued her journey, this time in the USA, to learn more about food - from mom-and-pop holes-in-the-wall to top-flight tasting menus. With an emerging knack for balancing flavours, she then threw herself into a restaurant internship where chefs offered guidance and, importantly, validation. That is what underpins Califarmication, her unique Orange County food truck devoted to farm-fresh, nutritious and delicious ingredients that power the human engine, not leave it comatose. It's a growing darling of vegetable-lovers and superfoods fans, especially vegetarians and vegans. The Newport Bowl is El's favourite take on what she ate growing up.

Follow them on
Instagram: @califarmication
Facebook: @califarmication

How to make it

🌿 SERVES 4

Ingredients
4 tsp vegetable oil
200g (8oz) spring onions, chopped
900g (2lb) yakisoba noodles (or another type)
350g (12oz) kale, shredded
115g (4oz) cabbage, shredded
150g (5oz) carrots, shredded
675g (1½lb) firm tofu
115g (4oz) pickled cabbage
115g (4oz) pickled daikon
16 cucumber slices
175g (6oz) mango, diced
175g (6oz) pineapple, diced
75g (3oz) peanuts
toasted sesame seeds
spring onions, finely chopped
coriander leaves, finely chopped

For the vinaigrette:
120ml (4fl oz) vinegar
120ml (4fl oz) water
4 tbs demerara sugar
3 tbs garlic puree
1 tbs sambal hot sauce
1 tbs Thai sweet chilli sauce
1 tsp vegetarian fish sauce
4 tsp coconut water
salt, to taste (optional)

Method
1. Heat the oil in a wok. Once it smokes, add the spring onions and noodles. Toss to coat and set aside off the heat.

2. To make the vinaigrette, put the vinegar, water and sugar in a small pan on medium heat and cook until the sugar dissolves. Stir in the garlic.

3. Once fragrant, turn off the heat and add the sambal, chilli sauce, fish sauce and coconut water. Add salt and more sugar, if desired.

4. In a large bowl, combine the hot noodles, kale, cabbage, carrots and tofu (or a cooked meat). Pour in 250ml (8fl oz) vinaigrette.

5. Toss together and pile on a plate.

6. To garnish, top with pickled cabbage and daikon, cucumbers, mango and pineapple. Pile peanuts in the middle and sprinkle with toasted sesame seeds, spring onion and coriander.

Paperboy

'On a sunny day, it's a banner day for us. Everybody wants to be outside... It's a real casual vibe.'
Ryan Harms, owner

BEC SANDWICH

PAPERBOY, AUSTIN, USA

For Ryan Harms running a food truck is all about quality: of life and of food. In the restaurant industry years before opening Paperboy in 2015 in East Austin, Harms knew he wanted to operate a business that allowed his team to enjoy the outdoors. That's a definite perk at his E 11th St location, which is open for breakfast and brunch. As for food quality, Harms seeks a one-two punch: a top-ingredient breakfast paired with amazing coffee. He sources locally as much as he can - the eggs on the signature BEC sandwich come from nearby Milagro Farm, and produce is plucked at Phoenix Farms in Bastrop. Local roaster Tweed provides the coffee. Almost everything is made from scratch inside the trailer - pickled vegetables, preserves, bread… As Harms confesses, 'We've pushed the limit of what's possible out of that thing.' Paperboy opened a second location in South Austin in 2017.

Follow them on
Instagram: @paperboyaustin
Facebook: www.facebook.com/paperboyaustin

How to make it

SERVES 1

Ingredients
2 thick-cut bacon rashers
1 egg
1 brioche or buttermilk bun
2–3 tbs pimiento cheese spread (see below)
salt & ground black pepper, to taste
seasonal greens, to garnish

For the pimiento cheese spread:
25g (1oz) mayonnaise
35g (1¼oz) red chilli sauce
25g (1oz) Havarti cheese, grated
25g (1oz) mature Cheddar cheese, grated
salt, to taste
vinegar, to taste

For the red chilli sauce (makes enough for several sandwiches):
10 dried guajillo chillies
1½ tbs rapeseed oil
6 garlic cloves, finely chopped
500g (1lb) onions, sliced
1 pickled jalapeño pepper
87.5ml (3fl oz) distilled white vinegar
salt, to taste

Method
1. For the chilli sauce, wearing gloves, remove the stems and seeds from the guajillo chillies. Toast in a frying pan for 1 minute, then set aside.

2. Heat the oil in a large pan over medium-high heat, add the garlic and fry until golden. Add the onion and sweat for 5 minutes. Add the guajillos and jalapeños and cook on low heat for 1 hour, checking occasionally. Add the vinegar and season with salt to taste.

3. Blend until smooth, adding a splash of water or vinegar, if needed. Chill.

4. Combine the ingredients for the pimiento cheese spread. Fry the bacon and egg, cooking and seasoning the egg to your taste.

5. Slice and toast the bun. Assemble the sandwich: bottom bun, pimiento cheese spread, bacon, red chilli sauce, egg, top bun. Add greens as a garnish or use in the sandwich.

THE VIET BANH MI

CHICAGO LUNCHBOX, CHICAGO, USA

John Nguyen launched Chicago Lunchbox in 2013. That he had no formal culinary background didn't stop him from buying a truck on Craigslist and rejigging it to cook dishes inspired by his Vietnamese-American childhood. Street food was his passion, and the bright orange truck was his way to bring quick, sriracha-fired bites of goodness to hungry Chicagoans all over town. It was a good move, and a second truck has now hit the streets, and a bricks-and-mortar Lunchbox has opened downtown. The bánh mì sandwich is Lunchbox's staple. You can get it the traditional way with Vietnamese grilled pork - aka 'the Viet' - but Nguyen also makes inspired mash-ups using Korean barbecue beef, Thai basil chicken and Filipino sweet sausage. And if spicy meat and pickled veggies on a warm, crunchy baguette isn't your thing, you can get them in a rice box, noodle box, tortilla or salad bowl.

Follow them on
Twitter/Instagram: @chicagolunchbox

How to make it

SERVES 2

Ingredients
220g (7½oz) pork shoulder, sliced 3mm (⅛in) thick
2 French baguettes, halved lengthways & toasted

For the marinade:
30g (1oz) sugar
½ tsp ground black pepper
1 shallot
2 tsp finely chopped lemongrass
1 tbs finely chopped garlic
1 tbs soy sauce
2½ tbs oyster sauce
1½ tbs fish sauce
2½ tbs rice wine

For the pickled daikon & carrot:
1 carrot, shredded
½ small Japanese daikon, shredded
2½ tbs distilled vinegar
30g (1oz) sugar

For the spicy mayo sauce:
2 tsp sriracha chilli sauce
30g (1oz) mayonnaise
½ garlic clove, finely chopped

For the sandwich toppings:
small handful cucumber, sliced
small handful red onion, chopped
small bunch coriander leaves, chopped
½ jalapeño pepper, sliced (optional)

Method
1. Mix together all ingredients for the marinade. Pour over the pork and massage it in. Cover and refrigerate for at least 4–5 hours (preferably overnight).

2. Combine the ingredients for the pickled daikon and carrot and leave to sit for an hour.

3. Combine the ingredients for the spicy mayo sauce.

4. Lift the meat out of the marinade. Heat a frying pan, add the pork and cook on medium high for 2–3 minutes, until the meat is fully cooked (it can also be grilled). You'll need to do this in batches.

5. Place a generous quantity of meat in each toasted baguette. Top with pickled daikon and carrot, cucumber, red onion, coriander and jalapeño, then drizzle with spicy mayo sauce.

home of Grandpa John's *famous*
waffles, chicken and ribs

"I was in my daughter's house about 3 years ago, fixing waffles, and she said, "You know what, dad?" - and people have been telling me this for years – "you need to start a restaurant.""
'Grandpa' John Fleischmann, co-owner

Call 615.4

Pork Slider
w/ fries
$9.33

Smoked
Wings

Fr
$2

BLUE CHEESE SLAW

BANJO'S, NASHVILLE, USA

Four decades ago, John Fleischmann started making waffles for his kids after church on Sunday mornings. The waffles were good - really good. Pretty soon, the kids started inviting their friends over. Then their friends started inviting their parents. Before he knew it, Fleischmann was making waffles for 30 or 40 people every weekend. Today, Fleischmann and his family cook up his famous waffles - and fried chicken, pulled pork, blue cheese slaw, sweet potato biscuits and other homestyle favourites - for far more people than that. They own Banjo's Food Truck, whose retro plaid paint job has become a welcome site around Nashville, Tennessee since it opened in 2016. The chicken and waffles, served up with a warm drizzle of maple syrup, is a bestseller, while regulars go gaga for the unique blue cheese slaw. 'Even if you don't like blue cheese, you'll love the blue cheese slaw,' says Fleischmann, who prefers to go by 'Grandpa John.' Tennessee visitors eager to sink their teeth into Grandpa John's crispy-on-the-outside, creamy-on-the-inside waffles, shattery-crusted fried chicken and salty, savory slaw can find Banjo's tooling around Music City - or visit its new bricks-and-mortar location.

Follow them on
Instagram: @banjosfoodtruck

How to make it

🌿 SERVES A CROWD

Ingredients

1½L (48fl oz) mayonnaise
350ml (12fl oz) cider vinegar
3 tbs black pepper
3 tbs sugar
1½ tbs prepared horseradish
3 tsp salt
1½ tsp cayenne
240ml (8fl oz) lemon juice
2kg (4.5lbs) shredded green and red cabbage and carrots
250g (8oz) crumbled blue cheese
24 spring onion tops, cut into ½cm (¼in) pieces
220g (4oz) sugar

Method

1. Mix first eight ingredients well and refrigerate for 12 hours. This makes a batch of Alabama white barbecue sauce.

2. Combine cabbage and carrot mix, spring onions and blue cheese and mix well.

3. Combine 700ml (25fl oz) of the Alabama white barbecue sauce with the sugar and mix well, then pour over the cabbage mix and toss until well coated.

4. Allow slaw to sit for at least 4 hours before serving.

OLD-FASHIONED PEACH CAKE

with peach cream cheese frosting

THE PEACH TRUCK, NASHVILLE, USA

For peach lovers in Nashville, the emerald-green 1964 jeep is a welcome sight. Starting each June, the truck rambles around town, its bed full of luscious, delicately fragrant peaches. The brainchild of Stephen and Jessica Rose, the Peach Truck has been running since 2012, and since then the fruits have starred in some of the finest pies, preserves and glazes in the mid-South. 'I grew up in Peach County, Georgia, and I just had this nostalgia for summer and peaches on the front porch,' Rose says. 'Moving to Nashville, I couldn't figure out why we didn't have those great peaches.' After all, Tennessee shares a border with Georgia. So, the Roses began hauling truckloads from a farm in Fort Valley, nicknamed 'Peach City'. They sell over 40 varieties, from the aromatic White Lady to tarter freestone varieties, perfect for canning. What will they have when you visit? Whatever's freshest, of course.

Follow them on
Instagram: @thepeachtruck
Facebook: www.facebook.com/thepeachtruck

152

How to make it

🌱 SERVES 16

Ingredients

400g (14oz) plain flour, plus extra
    for dusting
½ tsp salt
3¾ tsp baking powder
175g (6oz) salted butter, softened
450g (1lb) granulated sugar
3 large eggs
1 tsp vanilla extract
½ tsp almond extract
250ml (8fl oz) washed, pitted &
    pureed peaches
peach slices, to garnish (optional)

For the frosting:

3 washed, pitted peaches
1 tbs granulated sugar
225g (8oz) full-fat cream cheese,
    softened
115g (4oz) salted butter,
    softened
450g (1lb) icing sugar
½ tsp vanilla extract

Method

1. Preheat the oven to 180°C (350°F).

2. Grease three 20cm (8in) round cake tins, line the bottoms with baking parchment and dust the sides lightly with flour.

3. Puree the peaches in a blender and set aside.

4. Sift together the flour, salt and baking powder.

5. In the bowl of an electric mixer fitted with a paddle attachment, beat the butter, sugar, eggs, vanilla and almond extract for 3 minutes, scraping down the sides as needed.

6. Add the flour a little at a time, alternating with peach puree.

7. Beat for 2 minutes, scraping the bowl halfway.

8. Divide the batter equally among the tins and spread evenly.

9. Bake for 25–30 minutes, until inserting a skewer in the middle comes out clean. Cool on wire racks.

10. For the frosting, put the peaches and granulated sugar in a blender and process until smooth.

11. Put the peach puree into a pan over medium-high heat and cook, stirring constantly, until reduced to a thick paste. Cool completely.

12. Put the cream cheese and butter in the mixer and beat with the paddle attachment to combine.

13. Add the icing sugar slowly, scraping the sides as needed.

14. Add the vanilla and peach paste and beat on high for another minute, until fluffy.

15. Assemble the cake one layer at a time, spreading about one-quarter of the frosting on each of the bottom two layers.

16. Apply a thin coating of frosting all over the top and outside and refrigerate for 1 hour to set before spreading the remaining frosting evenly over the top and sides.

17. Chill for 1 hour, then garnish with fresh peaches if you like.

ALABAMA TAILGATERS

FIDEL GASTRO'S, TORONTO, CANADA

Matt Basile left a career as an advertising copywriter to dive into the food world, launching Fidel Gastro's in Canada's largest city in 2012. Why Fidel Gastro's? 'I just thought the name was cool,' Basile says. 'I guess that was the copywriter in me.' Next came a gig as host of a reality TV show, Rebel Without a Kitchen, which chronicled the truck's development; a 2014 book, Street Food Diaries; and a bricks-and-mortar restaurant, Lisa Marie. Through it all, Fidel Gastro's continues to dish out eclectic creations like the 'Gorgeous Jorge' (peanut butter pulled pork with bacon jam), 'El Paisano' (meatballs with tomato sauce and a spaghetti patty), and these 'Alabama Tailgaters' (bacon-wrapped beef balls stuffed with cheese and kimchi).

Follow them on
Instagram: @fidelgastros
Twitter: @fidelgastros

How to make it

SERVES 5

Ingredients
10 slices thin-cut bacon
10 slices beef carpaccio
1 tsp kosher salt
1 tsp ground black pepper
4 tbs grated mozzarella cheese
50g (2oz) finely chopped kimchi
1 bunch coriander leaves, finely chopped
120ml (4 fl oz) sriracha aioli (below)

For sriracha aioli:
4 egg yolks
1 lime
1l (1¾ pints) rapeseed oil
430ml (15fl oz) sriracha chilli sauce
salt, to taste

Method
1. To prepare the sriracha aioli, whisk egg yolks and lime juice together. Slowly pour in oil, drop by drop, and whisk continuously, waiting until the oil is incorporated to add more.

2. Fold in the sriracha. Add salt to taste. Set aside.

3. Preheat the oven to 180°C (350°F).

4. Cut each slice of bacon two-thirds of the way down. Use the smaller pieces to turn the bacon into 'T' shapes.

5. Place a slice of beef carpaccio where the two pieces of bacon cross. Lightly season.

6. Top the carpaccio with a pinch of cheese, kimchi and coriander.

7. Fold the two shorter ends of the bacon over the filling, then roll the longer part until you have a ball of bacon wrapped around the fillings.

8. In a pan, cook the balls over high heat for 4–5 minutes per side.

9. Transfer to a baking sheet and bake for 12 minutes, or until cheese oozes out and the balls are heated through.

10. Stick each ball on its own skewer or toothpick and serve with sriracha aioli.

155

NANNER S'MORE

MEGGROLLS, ALEXANDRIA, USA

Rave reviews for a creative party platter turned a quirky culinary side project into a full-blown career for Meghan 'Megg' Baroody, who has the magic touch when handling a deep-fryer. Her signature creation, the 'meggroll', is fun fusion food at its finest - a crunchy wonton shell that serves as the bread of a sandwich with unique fixings inside. Word spread among friends and acquaintances, and in 2013 she bought a food truck and started to sell her creations to the public. Over the years, Megg has refined a shortlist of recipes, including her take on a chicken parm, buffalo wings, mac and cheese, and our favourite, the Bigg Megg, which tastes uncannily like a Big Mac, but in an egg roll. Such was the truck's popularity, devotees would stalk it as it trundled around the suburb of Alexandria, so in 2017 Megg opened a brick-and-mortar option off King Street.

**Follow them on
Twitter:** @meggrollmania

How to make it

MAKES 10

Ingredients
75g (3oz) melted butter
200g (7oz) digestive biscuits
  (graham crackers)
150g (5oz) granulated sugar
pinch of kosher salt
5 large bananas, not too ripe
10 large egg roll wrappers
  (flour-based)
75g (1oz) dark chocolate chips
900ml (1½ pints) rapeseed oil
marshmallow fluff

Method
1. Gently melt the butter in a pan, then let it cool.

2. Buzz the crackers in a food processor until you have dust. Add 100g (3½oz) of the sugar and the salt and pulse briefly. Combine the crumbs and butter.

3. Cut the bananas into 7½cm (3½in)-long pieces, then roll them in the remaining sugar.

4. Place 1 wrapper on a surface with one corner pointing towards you. Spread 3 tbs of the crumble to cover a 7½cm (3in)-diameter circular area. Sprinkle 12–15 chocolate chips on top, then place the banana horizontally on top.

5. Wet the top corners of the wrapper. Wrap the corner pointing towards you around the banana, roll the wrapper away from you, then fold the sides inwards and seal the top. Repeat with the remaining wrappers and ingredients, reserving some of the crumble.

6. Heat the oil in a large, heavy pan over medium-high heat, until a cube of bread browns in about 45 seconds.

7. Deep-fry the rolls a couple at a time for 3–5 minutes, until golden, then drain on kitchen paper while you cook the next batch.

8. Cut each roll in half and top with marshmallow fluff. If you have a blowtorch, char the fluff, then sprinkle with more of the crumble and serve.

157

RED VELVET COOKIES

CAPTAIN COOKIE AND THE MILK MAN, WASHINGTON DC, USA

Ever since baking his first chocolate chip cookie aged four, Kirk Francis has been trying to achieve the perfect recipe. His mission continues. In 2012, he and his wife Juliann started a food truck business, Captain Cookie and the Milk Man. Kirk converted their four trucks into mini-bakeries and his uncle hand-painted their exteriors; quirkily, their first 'cookiemobile' was a former Washington Post delivery van. These days, the cookiemobiles set up shop throughout DC, Virginia, and Maryland (and there are two bricks-and-mortar locations). Every morning within the compact kitchens the duo and their staff whip up eight cookie flavours, including chocolate chip, double chocolate, oatmeal raisin and ginger molasses - plus weekly experiments like the red velvet cookie. Enjoy these fresh, chewy bites with natural ice cream; the ice-cream cookie sandwich is their best-seller. The company also 'saves the world one cookie at a time' by supporting food charities in Washington DC.

Follow them on Twitter: @captaincookiedc

How to make it

MAKES 20

Ingredients

160g (5½oz) unsalted butter, softened
130g (4½oz) white sugar
115g (4oz) soft light brown sugar
1 tbs red food colouring
5 tbs milk
1 tsp vanilla extract
25g (1oz) unsweetened cocoa powder
1 tsp bicarb soda (baking soda)
1 tsp baking powder
½ tsp sea salt
210g (7½oz) plain flour
75g (3oz) white chocolate chips

Method

1. Preheat the oven to 200°C (400°F).

2. Using a stand mixer or hand beater, cream the butter and sugars together on medium speed until light and fluffy (about 3–5 minutes).

3. Mix in the food colouring, milk and vanilla.

4. In a separate bowl, stir together the cocoa powder, bicarb soda, baking powder, salt and flour.

5. Add the flour mixture to the butter mixture and mix on low until well combined, scraping the sides of the bowl occasionally.

6. Mix in the chocolate chips. Scoop the dough by rounded tablespoons on to an ungreased baking sheet and bake for 11–12 minutes, or until the cookies are slightly puffed and crackled on top.

7. Remove and place on a wire rack to cool.

159

'We try to make a good combination of flavours. And our secret to really good taste? Fresh ingredients and a lot of love.'
Giuseppe Lanzone,
owner

PERUVIAN PAN CON CHICHARRÓN

PERUVIAN BROTHERS, WASHINGTON DC, USA

When a logo depicts a *chollo* (Peruvian hat) and two men in a boat, you know there's a story. Giuseppe and Mario Lanzone, owners of Peruvian Brothers, spent their infancies in Peru before moving to the USA. Giuseppe was a two-time Olympic rower, while Mario worked on Mediterranean yachts. On reuniting in DC, they started a food truck company in 2013 using a former mail delivery vehicle. These days, three trucks roam the streets of DC and surrounds, serving up food that Mario prepares in their catering kitchen. The offerings are a nod to their Peruvian heritage: quinoa salad, empanadas and *arroz arabe*, a wild rice mix, served with meat. The fan favourite, *pan con chicharrón* (roasted pork in a bun), has a fascinating past: around 1492, upon landing in South America with pigs, the Spanish took a liking to the combination of salty pork and the local sweet potato.

Follow them on Twitter: @perubrothers

How to make it

SERVES 4/6

Ingredients
4–6 freshly baked buns/rolls

For the chicharrón
4L (7 pints) boiling water
1 tbs salt
1 tbs ground black pepper
1 tbs ground cumin
1 tbs achiote paste
1 tbs garlic puree
1 tbs dried oregano
½ medium red onion
675g (1½lb) pork tenderloin
2.5L (4¼ pints) rapeseed oil (or enough to cover the pork)

For the sweet potato slices:
1 sweet potato

For the criolla sauce:
1 medium red onion, finely diced
2 tbs white vinegar
2 tbs olive oil
2 tbs freshly squeezed lime juice
½ diced orange pepper
2 tbs chopped parsley
salt and ground black pepper, to taste

Method
1. For the *chicharrón*, bring the water to a boil with all the ingredients except the pork and oil. Once boiling, add the pork and boil for 20 minutes.

2. Remove and drain very well on kitchen paper, patting as dry as you can.

3. Preheat the oven to 220°C (425°F) and bake the sweet potato for 20 minutes, then peel and cut into 5mm (¼in) slices.

4. Heat the oil for the pork in a deep, heavy pan to 200°C (400°F), lower in the pork and deep-fry for 5 minutes. Remove to kitchen paper to drain.

5. Add the potato slices to the hot oil and deep-fry until golden, then drain on kitchen paper.

6. To make the criolla sauce, combine the ingredients.

7. Cut the pork into 5mm (¼in) slices.

8. Halve each bun/roll, add some sweet potato slices and pork and top with criolla sauce.

161

FISH TACOS

LOS VIAJEROS, NEW YORK CITY, USA

Neither Caitlyn Napolitano nor her co-conspirator, boyfriend and breakdance partner Carlos Dacosta had any professional culinary experience when they rolled out Los Viajeros, a purveyor of quality Latin fusion specialties - tacos, burritos and quesadillas - at locations throughout New York City. But that, says Napolitano, is the beauty of a food truck. Anyone with passion, gumption and a love of cooking can do it. And it's how, starting in 2015, in search of a business to call their own, they followed their families' advice, embraced Dacosta's Dominican roots (and family recipes!) and Napolitano's love of Latin flavours, and did just that. The result? After a period of intense learning, Dacosta appeared on Rachel Ray. Then Napolitano won Food Network's Chopped in 2017. And now, in addition to their brightly painted truck, they're opening a permanent store in an underground market near Central Park. Both will carry their best-selling fish tacos, based on a recipe from Dacosta's grandmother.

Follow them on
Instagram: @los_viajeros_foodtruck
Twitter: @los_viajeros_foodtruck

How to make it

SERVES 4/6

Ingredients
115g (4oz) plain flour
1 tbs paprika
½ tbs cayenne pepper
½ tbs garlic powder
1 tbs salt
½ tbs ground black pepper
900g (2lb) tilapia fillets
vegetable oil
16 x 15cm (6in) corn tortillas
1 lime, cut into 16 wedges

For the cabbage slaw:
115g (4oz) mayonnaise
juice of ½ lime
splash of vinegar
½ tsp ground cumin
¼ head of red cabbage, shredded
¼ head of green cabbage, shredded
salt and ground black pepper, to taste

For the pico de gallo:
200g (7oz) plum tomatoes, diced
50g (2oz) red onion, diced
4 tbs coriander leaves, chopped
½ mango, cut into chunks
1 tbs lime juice
salt and ground black pepper, to taste

For the chipotle mayo:
65g (2½oz) chipotle peppers, chopped
175g (6oz) mayonnaise

Method
1. In a bowl, combine the slaw ingredients and set aside to marinate for 30 minutes.

2. In another bowl, combine the pico de gallo ingredients. Set aside.

3. In a third bowl, blend the chipotle peppers and mayonnaise until smooth. Set aside.

4. Combine the flour, paprika, cayenne pepper, garlic powder, salt and pepper in a shallow dish, then turn the tilapia in the mixture to coat.

5. Fill a large sauté pan with 5cm (2in) of oil and heat to 180°C (350°F). Submerge and fry the tilapia in the oil for 3 minutes.

6. Heat the tortillas for a minute on each side in a frying pan, then move to a plate and divide the tilapia across them. Cover each with slaw, some pico de gallo, a splodge of chipotle mayo and a lime wedge.

© BRIAN DAVID

'The most important thing is to go out there every day. My customers are the coolest people. I love to serve them. I eat at my truck every day and they do too.'
Nicko Karagiorgos, owner

PORK SOUVLAKI

UNCLE GUSSY'S, NEW YORK CITY, USA

Brothers Nicko and Franky Karagiorgos were born into the business of vending street food. For as long as they can remember, their uncles were pushing carts and selling hotdogs, sausages or souvlaki near their childhood home in Astoria, Queens, and they loved to help. So, after dabbling in corporate America, they jumped at an opportunity in 2009 to take over a plum Park Avenue location from their Uncle Gus. First, they built a larger, walk-in cart and then upgraded to a truck. Today, they have two Uncle Gussy's trucks, a restaurant and online ordering, but haven't sacrificed the quality and attention to detail - fresh, natural meats and vegetables, prepared by hand - that keep lines long and customers raving. Because, to them, it's the little things that count, including a commitment to charity work in support of kids and health causes. Nicko's personal favourite dish is this Greek classic: pork souvlaki.

Follow them on
Instagram: @unclegussys
Twitter: @UncleGussys

How to make it

SERVES 6

Ingredients
675g (1½lb) boneless pork loin
    or tenderloin, cut into
    1cm (½in) cubes
120ml (4fl oz) red table wine
115g (4oz) red onion, finely
    chopped
2 tbs oregano (ideally Greek)
¼ tsp salt
¼ tsp ground black pepper
50ml (2 tbs) olive oil
50ml (2 tbs) lemon juice
225g (8oz) tzatziki
6 Greek pittas
1 large tomato, chopped

Method
1. Prepare the marinade by mixing together the wine, half the onion, 1 tbs oregano, and a pinch of salt and pepper in a bowl.

2. Add the pork, stir to coat, cover and refrigerate overnight.

3. When ready to cook, light a barbecue or preheat a grill.

4. Combine the olive oil, lemon juice and remaining oregano, salt and pepper.

5. Thread the pork on to six skewers and brush with the marinade.

6. Cook over the flames or under the grill for 8–12 minutes until a tiny bit of pink remains inside, turning as it cooks.

7. Dip the meat into the oil mix.

8. Spread tzatziki on each pitta, add cooked pork, tomato chunks and the remaining onion.

167

CHILLI CON CORNE WAFFLE

WAFELS & DINGES, NEW YORK CITY, USA

When Thomas DeGeest moved from Belgium to the USA, he fell in love with New York City and joined the corporate mainstream. After 12 years, though, feeling burned out, he tapped a passion for his homeland's waffles and, in 2007, launched Wafels & Dinges, the self-styled Belgian Ministry of Culinary Affairs' Department of Wafels. Eleven years later, there are two trucks, two cafes, five kiosks and six carts selling freshly cooked Belgian-style waffles loaded with delicious toppings (the 'dinges'). The sugary Liege Wafel - the ones 'Belgians kept secret' when waffles became an American sensation after the 1964 New York World's Fair - is the soft and crunchy platform for a variety of sweet dinges, but there are also savoury classics, like the Chilli con Corne, a cornmeal treat that's like a Belgian take on Tex-Mex. True to the company mantra that 'All the world is a wafel, and all of us are merely dinges', it makes an appearance each winter, just when most desired.

**Follow them on
Instagram:** @wafflesanddinges

How to make it

SERVES 4

Ingredients
For the batter:
60g (2oz) plain flour
125g (4½oz) yellow corn meal
60g (2oz) dark brown muscovado sugar
1 tsp salt
pinch of ground black pepper
pinch of dried chilli flakes
pinch of ground coriander
pinch of chilli powder
½ tsp ground cumin
225ml (8fl oz) single cream
1 egg
25ml (1fl oz) rapeseed oil
100g (3½oz) corn, drained
½ tbs honey
25g (1oz) baking powder

For the topping:
mature Cheddar cheese, grated
hot beef chilli
dollop of sour cream
coriander leaves

Method
1. In a large bowl, combine the dry batter ingredients: flour, corn meal, sugar, salt, pepper, chilli flakes, coriander, chilli powder and cumin.

2. In a separate bowl, mix together the wet ingredients: cream, egg, oil, corn and honey.

3. Stir the wet ingredients into the dry to make the batter. This can be refrigerated for up to 3 days.

4. When you are ready to cook, mix in the baking powder. Preheat a waffle iron.

5. Pour enough batter to cover the surface of the waffle iron and cook each waffle for about 3 minutes.

6. Remove to a plate and allow to crisp for 2 minutes.

7. To serve, add toppings to taste.

'How did we get the idea
for The Duck Truck?
We're a little crazy.'
Isabelle Pelletier,
co-owner

BARLEY RISOTTO

with duck confit and mushrooms

THE DUCK TRUCK, MONTRÉAL, QUÉBEC, CANADA

Everything's just ducky at this Montréal food truck that serves canard in many forms, from 'Quack 'n' cheese' (macaroni and cheese topped with duck confit) and 'Empanaduck' (duck empanadas) to this risotto made from barley, mushrooms, herbs and more confit duck. The Duck Truck is the brainchild of Isabelle Pelletier and Thierry Baron, who also runs Montréal's Vertige restaurant. 'They realised that duck was a versatile meat that they could use to prepare many different dishes, rather than being locked into a single concept. No other Montréal food truck was serving duck, and since the meat is not inexpensive', Pelletier quips, 'we were sure that no one else would do this.' Pelletier says that they also took inspiration from Wilensky's Light Lunch, known for its pressed sandwiches. After envisioning a similarly iconic sandwich made from duck, they invented their own, 'Le Vilain', stuffed with braised duck, onions and Cheddar.

Follow them on
Instagram: @ducktruckmtl
Twitter: @TheDuckTruck1

How to make it

SERVES 8 AS A SIDE DISH OR 4 AS A MAIN DISH

Ingredients

1.3L (2¼ pints) chicken broth
2 tsp butter
4 tsp olive oil
1 white onion, finely chopped
250g (9oz) pearl barley
120ml (4fl oz) port
200g (7oz) mushrooms (shiitake, oyster, white, or an assortment), roughly chopped
4 confit duck legs, meat pulled and shredded
50g (2oz) grated Parmesan cheese
juice of ½ lemon
salt and ground black pepper, to taste
chopped parsley and/or chopped chives (optional), to taste
fresh rocket (optional), to garnish

Method

1. Put 1L (1¾ pints) broth in a pan and bring to the boil.

2. In a large pan, heat 1 tsp butter and 1 tsp oil over low heat until the butter is melted. Add the onion and sauté for 1–2 minutes to soften, but not brown.

3. Add the barley and stir to coat with fat. The grains should whiten and become slightly translucent.

4. Add the port and raise the heat to reduce the liquid, then pour in the broth. Season.

5. Bring to the boil, then reduce the heat, cover and simmer for 20–25 minutes.

6. Spread out the barley on a plate.

7. Heat the remaining oil in a frying pan and sauté the mushrooms for 5 minutes, until softened.

8. Put the remaining 300ml (½ pint) broth in a pan and bring to the boil. Stir in the barley, mushrooms and duck.

9. Cook, stirring, adding more broth if necessary, until the barley is cooked.

10. To serve, stir in the cheese, remaining 1 tsp butter, lemon juice, seasoning and herbs, if using. Garnish with rocket.

171

INDEX

TYPE OF DISH

ACKNOWLEDGEMENTS

Published in March 2019
by Lonely Planet Global Limited
CRN 554153
www.lonelyplanet.com
ISBN 978 17886 8131 5
© Lonely Planet 2019

Printed in China
10 9 8 7 6 5 4 3 2 1

Managing Director, Publishing Piers Pickard
Associate Publisher Robin Barton
Commissioning Editor Christina Webb
Editing Lucy Doncaster, Dora Ball
Proofing Karyn Noble
Art Direction Daniel Di Paolo
Design Tina García
Picture Research Regina Wolek, Aisha Zia
Print Production Nigel Longuet

Written by Kate Armstrong, Amy Balfour, Dora Ball, Ryan Barrell, Andrew Bender, Joshua Samuel Brown, Penny Carroll, Lucy Corne, Stephanie d'Arc Taylor, Jane D'Arcy, Ksenia Elzes, Dale De Almeida, Esme Fox, Ethan Gelber, Analia Glogowski, Chris Griffiths, Deepika Gumaste, Carolyn B. Heller, Emily Henley, Yoana Hristova, Tom Le Mesurier, Sofia Levin, Clementine Logan, James Gabriel Martin, Heather Mason, Emily Matchar, Karyn Noble, Lorna Parkes, Monique Perrin, Brandon Presser, Chitra Ramaswamy, Charles Rawlings-Way, Agnes Rivera, Macca Sherifi, Tom Spurling, Jennifer Walker, Hahna Yoon, Karla Zimmerman.

Thanks to Imogen Bannister, Alex Butler, Neill Coen, Jess Cole, Joe Davis, Jay Francis, Emily Frost, Alex Howard, Amy Lysen, Flora Macqueen, Fin McCarthy, Kat Nelson, Caroline Nowell, Niamh O'Brien, Kathryn Rowan, Ellie Simpson, Emma Sparks, Saralinda Turner, Art Witczak.

STAY IN TOUCH lonelyplanet.com/contact

AUSTRALIA
The Malt Store, Level 3, 551 Swanston St, Carlton, Victoria 3053 T: 03 8379 8000

IRELAND
Digital Depot, Roe Lane (off Thomas St), Digital Hub, Dublin 8, D08 TCV4

USA
124 Linden St, Oakland, CA 94607
T: 510 250 6400

UNITED KINGDOM
240 Blackfriars Rd, London SE1 8NW
T: 020 3771 5100

Although the authors and Lonely Planet have taken all reasonable care in preparing this book, we make no warranty about the accuracy or completeness of its content and, to the maximum extent permitted, disclaim all liability from its use.

Front cover images (left to right): © Colin Ross, © The Cheese Truck, © Greek Street Food, © Princess Kitchen
Contents page images (left to right): ©John Valls, © Mama Rocks Gourmet Burger, © Mama Rocks Gourmet Burger, ©John Valls, © Heisser Hobel, © Luis Garcia, © Luis Garcia, © Monira Kamal
Back cover images (top to bottom): © Jessica Lindsay, © Todd Winters, © John Valls

MIX
Paper from responsible sources
FSC™ C021741
www.fsc.org

Paper in this book is certified against the Forest Stewardship Council™ standards. FSC™ promotes environmentally responsible, socially beneficial and economically viable management of the world's forests.